For fifty years *Basic Christianity* has exposed the backbone of the Christian faith. Its uncompromising clarity, intelligent logic and easy application make this one of the most enduring of Christian classics. In a time of ambiguity and confusion I can think of no other book I would rather recommend. Every evangelist should consider *Basic Christianity* a masterclass in communicating the gospel. This book is a must-read for those who are seeking God, those wishing to refresh their own faith, or those who hope to lead others into the loving arms of Jesus Christ.

Rev. William Van Der Hart, evangelist and pastor

Lucid, clear and compelling. After *Mere Christianity*, perhaps no other book has helped more people come to faith. I'm thrilled that this classic has been appropriately shaped and refreshed for a modern audience without losing any of its timeless charm and persuasive brilliance. Having led and organized university missions for over twenty-five years I was sobered to be reminded of what a debt we all owe to this book and its author. 'Christ is Christianity' and no other book exemplifies a Christ-centred apologetic more simply and clearly.

Rev. Richard Cunningham, Director of UCCF: The Christian Unions

We can thank God that in the past few years those committed to Christian orthodoxy have been realizing the importance of the subjective and experiential aspects of the Christian gospel and using these in introducing Christianity to others. But the danger is that we can get so carried away by this that we forget the heart of what Christianity is all about. At such times it is good to go back to tried and tested expositions that have stood the test of time. And what better resource is there for this than John Stott's classic *Basic Christianity*?

Ajith Fernando, National Director, Youth for Christ, Sri Lanka

Clear, penetrating and fresh, *Basic Christianity* has everything that you want to say to someone who wants to know what Christianity is all about. With an engaging and accessible style, John Stott lays out the truth of the gospel. The account of the Bible's message is wonderfully straightforward and the challenge to respond to Jesus Christ is compelling. By the time you've read the first few pages you'll already be thinking of people to give this book to: don't pull back!
Rev. Dominic Smart, Gilcomston South Church, Aberdeen

This was the classic forerunner of strong, balanced evangelistic books, and I am delighted it is being republished fifty years later. It led many to faith then, and it will again.
Canon Dr Michael Green

Anything John Stott says is worth listening to ... anything he writes is worth reading. *Basic Christianity* is not only a classic 'must-read' for every believer, it is truly a blessing preserved on the written page for the enrichment of this generation, and those to come.
Anne Graham Lotz, author and speaker

John Stott's books have helped millions around the world to a better understanding of the Christian faith. I, for one, am extremely grateful for the way in which he explains complex and difficult issues with great clarity, insight and wisdom. *Basic Christianity* has become a classic of our time.
Nicky Gumbel, Vicar of Holy Trinity Brompton and pioneer of the Alpha course

[This slim volume] has introduced more people to Christ than any book I know other than the Bible.
Jim Sire, author

John Stott

Basic
Christianity

new edition

Inter-Varsity Press
Norton Street, Nottingham NG7 3HR, England
Email: ivp@ivpbooks.com
Website: www.ivpbooks.com

First published 1958
Reprinted 2009, 2010

British Library Cataloguing in Publication Data
A catalogue record for this book is available from the British Library.

ISBN: 978–1–84474–304–9

Set in Adobe Garamond
Typeset in Great Britain by CRB Associates, Potterhanworth, Lincolnshire
Printed and bound in Great Britain by Ashford Colour Press Ltd, Gosport,
Hampshire

Inter-Varsity Press publishes Christian books that are true to the Bible and that
communicate the gospel, develop discipleship and strengthen the church for its
mission in the world.

Inter-Varsity Press is closely linked with the Universities and Colleges
Christian Fellowship, a student movement connecting Christian Unions in
universities and colleges throughout Great Britain, and a member movement
of the International Fellowship of Evangelical Students. Website:
www.uccf.org.uk

All John Stott's royalties from this book have been irrevocably assigned to Langham Literature (formerly the Evangelical Literature Trust). Langham Literature is a programme of the Langham Partnership International (LPI), founded by John Stott. Chris Wright is the International Ministries Director.

Langham Literature distributes evangelical books to pastors, theological students and seminary libraries in the Majority World, and fosters the writing and publishing of Christian literature in many regional languages. For further information on Langham Literature, and the other programmes of LPI, visit the website at www.langhampartnership.org.

In the USA, the national member of the Langham Partnership International is John Stott Ministries. Visit the JSM website at www.johnstott.org.

CONTENTS

PART FOUR: HOW TO RESPOND

If you would like to run a *Basic Christianity* course, downloadable resources are available from www.ivpbooks.com/basicchristianity.

FOREWORD

There are a few landmark books that everyone in the world should read. This is one of the rare few.

In the twenty-first century, you cannot afford to ignore this book! Whether you are a sceptic, raised in another faith, a spiritual seeker or a Christian believer, you need to know why 2.3 billion people call themselves 'Christians'. You need to know what they believe and why they believe it.

This book is especially essential for leaders in business, government, academia, media, entertainment, journalism and other fields that work directly with people. To be able to have an intelligent conversation with one-third of our world's population, you need to understand their worldview.

John Stott's *Basic Christianty* is a classic introduction to the faith that has transformed billions of lives.

Rick Warren
Pastor, Saddleback Church

PREFACE TO THE FIFTIETH-ANNIVERSARY EDITION

Every three years a mission is held in Cambridge University, and one such took place in November 1952. Invited to be the chief missioner, I knew that my responsibilities would include giving a series of eight evening addresses in Great St Mary's, the university church. I also understood that a university mission would present a wonderful, if daunting, opportunity to lay before the university a systematic unfolding of the gospel, including the divine-human person of Jesus, the significance of his death and the evidence for his resurrection, the paradox of our humanness, made in God's image but fallen and rebellious, the possibility of a new birth into a new life, the challenge of personal commitment and the cost of discipleship.

This foundation outline proved to be the first of fifty university missions, beginning with Cambridge, Oxford, Durham and London, continuing with so-called 'red brick' universities, then crossing the Atlantic for missions in American and Canadian universities, continuing in Australia and New Zealand, and culminating in a number of missions in the universities of Africa and Asia.

Of course the gospel outline developed as it reflected local situations and as repetition encouraged improvement. But out of this foundational material *Basic Christianity* was born. It has been used worldwide, both to lead people from many different cultures and situations to Christ, and to establish young Christians in their faith. For example, a major general wrote:

I was brought to the foot of the cross by your *Basic Christianity* which I was reading (in 1965) at 40,000 feet in an RAF aircraft! I have never ceased to be grateful and have passed on very many copies...

And a young woman wrote:

When I was in the sixth form at school (way back in 1971) I was searching for God whoever He was, and [for] a life with meaning and purpose ... A Christian teacher at school, knowing of my search, lent me *Basic Christianity*. I devoured the book! I was so excited for even though I had been confirmed I had never really understood the basic tenets of Christianity. I did not even really understand why Christ died.

But the publishers (IVP) and I have naturally wondered how best and most appropriately to celebrate the fiftieth anniversary of the publication of *Basic Christianity*.

It was obviously necessary to update the language, not least by use of a modern translation of the Bible, and to respond to sensitivities relating to gender. We are grateful to David Stone for taking care of these sensitivities. In many ways a new book seemed to be needed, or at least a radical revision of the original. But I feel I have already, in *Why I am a Christian* (IVP, 2004), made my own contemporary statement of the gospel and do not feel the need to write another, even if I could. Besides, *Basic Christianity* is something of a period piece. It reflects the cultures of its own day and needs to be allowed to remain itself. We hope and pray that God will use it as he has done in the past, all over the world.

I end with the words of a young man who wrote to me in 1988 as follows:

I regard myself as having a somewhat insecure and rootless background. My mother is Brazilian, of Italian extraction, and my father is English. In 1980 – still going through a severe adolescence – I went to Argentina. It was near the end of my time there that I experienced a marvellous change within me. I started to thirst to know the truth, whatever it might be. I read *Basic Christianity* ... the words seemed to bounce out at me from the page. I felt convinced I'd discovered the truth although as yet I didn't know that Jesus was God and that he was calling me to an intimate relationship with him. It was only later that year when I was back in England ... that I finally made a personal act of surrender to the Lord Jesus Christ.

John Stott
December 2007

INTRODUCTION

'Hostile to the church, friendly to Jesus Christ.' These words describe large numbers of people, especially the young, today.

They are opposed to anything which looks like an institution. They cannot stand the establishment and its entrenched privileges. And they reject the church – not without some justification – because they see it as hopelessly corrupted by such evils.

Yet what they have rejected is the contemporary church, not Jesus Christ himself. It is precisely because they see a contradiction between the founder of Christianity and the current state of the church he founded that they are so critical and hold back. The person and teaching of Jesus have not lost their appeal, however. For one thing, he was himself an anti-establishment figure, and some of his words had revolutionary overtones. His ideals appear to have been entirely honourable. He breathed love and peace wherever he went. And, for another thing, he always practised what he preached.

But was he *true*?

An appreciable number of people throughout the world are still brought up in Christian homes where the truth of Christ and of Christianity is assumed. But when their critical faculties develop and they begin to think for themselves, they find it easier to discard the religion of their childhood than to make the effort to investigate whether or not it is true.

Very many others do not grow up in a Christian environment. Instead they absorb the teaching of Islam, Hinduism or

Buddhism, or ways of thinking which have no room for God at all.

Yet both groups, if and when they read about Jesus, find that he holds a fascination they cannot easily escape.

So our starting point is the historical figure of Jesus of Nazareth. He certainly existed. There can be no reasonable doubt about that. His existence as an historical figure is vouched for by pagan as well as Christian writers.

And, whatever else may be said about him, he was also very much a human being. He was born, he grew, he worked and sweated, rested and slept, he ate and drank, suffered and died like other people. He had a real human body and real human emotions.

But can we really believe that he was also in some sense 'God'? Isn't the deity of Jesus a rather picturesque Christian superstition? Is there any evidence for this amazing Christian assertion that the carpenter of Nazareth was the unique Son of God?

This question is fundamental. We cannot dodge round it. We must be honest. If Jesus was not God in human flesh, then Christianity is thoroughly discredited. We are left with just another religion with some beautiful ideas and noble ethics; its unique distinctiveness is gone.

But there *is* evidence for the deity of Jesus – good, strong, historical, cumulative evidence; evidence to which an honest person can subscribe without committing intellectual suicide. There are the extravagant claims which Jesus made for himself, so bold and yet so unassuming. Then there is his unique character. His strength and gentleness, his uncompromising righteousness and tender compassion, his care for children and his love for those at the margins, his self-mastery and self-sacrifice have won the admiration of the world. What is more, his cruel death was not the end of him. It is claimed that he rose again from death, and the circumstantial evidence for his resurrection is most compelling.

But suppose Jesus was the Son of God – is basic Christianity merely an acceptance of this fact? No. Once persuaded of who he is, we must examine what he came to do. What did he intend to achieve? The Bible's answer is that he 'came into the world to save sinners'. Jesus of Nazareth is the heaven-sent Rescuer whom we all need. We need to be forgiven and brought into friendship with the all-holy God, from whom our sins have separated us. We need to be set free from our selfishness and given strength to live up to our ideals. We need to learn to love others, friend and enemy alike. This is the meaning of what we call 'salvation'. This is what Christ came to win for us by his death and resurrection.

So is basic Christianity the belief that Jesus is the Son of God who came to be the Saviour of the world? No, it is not even that. To accept that he is divine, to acknowledge our need of salvation, and to believe in the effectiveness of what he did for us are still not enough. Christianity is not just about what we *believe*; it's also about how we *behave*. Our intellectual belief may be beyond criticism; but we have to put our beliefs into practice.

What then must we do? We must commit ourselves, heart and mind, soul and will, home and life, personally and unreservedly to Jesus Christ. We must humble ourselves before him. We must trust in him as *our* Saviour and submit to him as *our* Lord; and then go on to take our place as loyal members of the church and responsible citizens in the community.

This is basic Christianity, the theme of this book. But before we start by looking at the evidence for Jesus Christ being divine, we need to pause in order to reflect on the right approach to take. The Christian claim is that we can find God in Jesus Christ. Examining this claim will be much more straightforward when we realize, firstly, that God is himself seeking us and, secondly, that we must ourselves seek God.

Chapter 1

THE RIGHT
APPROACH

'In the beginning God.' The first four words of the Bible are more than a way of launching the story of creation or introducing the book of Genesis. They supply the key which opens our understanding to the Bible as a whole. They tell us that the religion of the Bible is a religion in which God takes the initiative.

The point is that we can never take God by surprise. We can never anticipate him. He always makes the first move. He is always there 'in the beginning'. Before we existed, God took action. Before we decided to look for God, God had already been looking for us. The Bible isn't about people trying to discover God, but about God reaching out to find us.

Many people imagine God sitting comfortably on a distant throne, remote, aloof, uninterested, a God who doesn't really care for our needs and has to be badgered into taking action on our behalf. Such a view is completely wrong. The Bible reveals a God who, long before it even occurs to men and women to turn to him, while they are still lost in darkness and sunk in sin, takes the initiative, rises from his throne, lays aside his glory, and stoops to seek until he finds them.

This sovereign, forward-looking activity of God is seen in many ways. He has taken the initiative in *creation*, bringing the universe and everything in it into existence: 'In the beginning God created the heavens and the earth.' He has taken the initiative in what we call *revelation*, making known both his nature and his will to humanity: 'In the past God spoke to our forefathers through the prophets at many times and in various ways, but in these last days he has spoken to us by his Son...' He has taken the initiative in the rescue operation of *salvation*, coming in Jesus Christ to set men and women free from their sins: 'God ... has come and has redeemed his people.'[1]

God has created. God has spoken. God has acted. These statements of God's initiative in three different areas form a summary of the religion of the Bible. It is with the second and third that we shall be concerned in this book, because basic Christianity by definition begins with the historical figure of Jesus Christ. If God has spoken, his last and greatest word to the world is Jesus Christ. If God has acted, his noblest act is the redemption of the world through Jesus Christ.

God has spoken and acted in Jesus Christ. He has said something. He has done something. This means that Christianity is not just pious talk. It is neither a collection of religious ideas nor a catalogue of rules. It is a 'gospel' (i.e. good news) – in the apostle Paul's words 'the gospel of God ... regarding his Son ... Jesus Christ our Lord'.[2] It is not primarily an invitation for us to do anything; it is supremely a declaration of what God has done in Christ for human beings like ourselves.

GOD HAS SPOKEN

Human beings are insatiably inquisitive creatures. Our minds cannot rest. We are always prying into the unknown. We pursue knowledge with restless energy. Our lives are a voyage of discovery. We are always asking questions, exploring, investigating, researching. We never grow out of the child's constant cry of 'Why?'

When our minds begin to think about God, however, they are bewildered. We grope around in the dark. We flounder helplessly out of our depth. But this should come as no surprise. For surely God, whatever or whoever he may be, is infinite, while we are finite creatures. He is altogether beyond our understanding. Therefore our minds, wonderfully effective instruments though they are when it comes to scientific investigation, cannot immediately help us here. They cannot reach up into the infinite mind of God. There is no ladder to climb, only a vast, unmeasured gulf. Job, a character in the Bible, is challenged with the question, 'Can you find out the deep things of God?' The only answer is 'No'. It is impossible.

And that is how it would have stayed, had God not taken the initiative to help us. We would have remained forever agnostic, asking – just like Pontius Pilate at the trial of Jesus – 'What is truth?' but never staying for an answer, never daring to hope that we would receive one. We would be those who worship, for it is part of human nature to worship someone or something, but all our altars would be like the one the apostle Paul found in Athens, dedicated 'To an unknown god'.

But God has spoken. He has taken the initiative to make himself known. The Christian concept of revelation is essentially reasonable. The idea is that God has 'unveiled' to our minds what would otherwise have been hidden from them. Part of his revelation is in nature:

The heavens declare the glory of God;
>   the skies proclaim the work of his hands.

What may be known about God is plain to them [that is, human beings], because God has made it plain to them. For since the creation of the world God's invisible qualities – his eternal power and divine nature – have been clearly seen, being understood from what has been made.[3]

We call this God's 'general' revelation (because it is made to all people everywhere) or 'natural' revelation (because it is in nature). But it is not sufficient. Yes, it reveals his existence, and gives us hints of his divine power, glory and faithfulness. But if we are to come to know God personally, to have our sins forgiven and to enter into relationship with him, we need something which goes further. We need something which helps us find out how to get to know him for ourselves. God's disclosure of himself needs to include his holiness, his love and his power to save from sin. The wonderful truth is that God gives us this as well. We call this a 'special' revelation, because it was made to a special people (the nation of Israel) through special messengers (people who are identified as 'prophets' in the Old Testament and 'apostles' in the New).

It is also 'supernatural', because it was given through a process we call 'inspiration', and it found its chief expression in Jesus – in who he is and in what he has done.

The way in which the Bible explains and describes this revelation is simply to say that God has 'spoken'. Speech is what we ourselves use where we can in order to communicate with one another most straightforwardly. It is by our words that we let others know what is in our minds. This is even more true of God in his desire to reveal his infinite mind to our finite minds. Since, as the prophet Isaiah put it, his thoughts are higher than our thoughts – as much as the heavens are higher than the earth – we could never get to know those thoughts unless he clothed them in words. The way the Bible puts it is that 'the word of the Lord came' to many prophets, until at last Jesus Christ came, and 'the Word became flesh and made his dwelling among us'.[4]

Paul wrote to his Christian friends in the city of Corinth along similar lines: '. . . since in the wisdom of God the world through its wisdom did not know him, God was pleased through the foolishness of what was preached to save those who believe.' We come to know God, not through our own wisdom, but through God's word (identified by Paul here as 'what we preach'); not through our human reason, but through divine revelation. It is because God has made himself known in Christ that the Christian can boldly go to those who are agnostic or superstitious and say to them, just as Paul did to the Athenians on the Areopagus, 'What you worship as something unknown I am going to proclaim to you.'

Much of the controversy between science and religion has arisen through a failure to appreciate this point. Scientific methods are no use when it comes to religion. Scientific knowledge advances through observation and experiment. It works on data supplied to us by our five physical senses. But when we enquire into what lies beyond the observable universe, when we seek to reflect on the metaphysical, there is no data for us to make use of. We cannot touch, see or hear God directly. Yet the Christian faith is based on the assertion that there once was a time when he chose to speak, and to clothe himself with a body which could be seen and touched. So in the New Testament, John began his first letter with the claim, 'That which was from the beginning, which we have heard, which we have seen with our eyes, which we have looked at and our hands have touched . . . we proclaim to you . . . '

GOD HAS TAKEN ACTION

The Christian good news is not simply a declaration that God has *said* something. It also affirms that God has *done* something.

God has taken the initiative in both these ways because this is what we need. It isn't just that we are ignorant but also that we are sinful. This is why it isn't enough for God simply to reveal himself to us and dispel our ignorance. He must also take action to save us from our sins. He began in Old Testament days. He called Abraham from his home in Ur, making him and his descendants into a nation, rescuing them from slavery in Egypt, entering into a covenant with them at Mount Sinai, leading them across the desert into the Promised Land, guiding and teaching them as his special people.

All this was by way of preparation for his even greater deed of redemption in Christ. People needed to be delivered, not from slavery in Egypt or from exile in Babylon, but from the bondage and alienation of sin. It was chiefly for this that Jesus Christ came. He came as a Saviour.

> . . . You are to give him the name Jesus, because he will save his people from their sins.

> Here is a trustworthy saying that deserves full acceptance: Christ Jesus came into the world to save sinners.

> For the Son of Man came to seek and to save what was lost.

He was like the shepherd in the parable told by Jesus who missed the only sheep which was lost from the flock and went out to search until he found it.[5]

Christianity is a religion of salvation, and the fact is that there is nothing in any of the non-Christian religions to compare with this message of a God who loved, and came after, and died for, a world of lost sinners.

OUR RESPONSE

God has spoken. God has taken action. The record and interpretation of these divine words and deeds is to be found in the Bible. The problem for many people is that this is where they remain. It's all too easy to imagine that what God has said and done is all in the past and just leave it at that. But it needs to come out of history into experience, out of the Bible into life. God has spoken – but have we listened to his word? God has acted – but have we benefited from what he has done?

God has spoken – but have we listened to his word? God has acted – but have we benefited from what he has done?

What we must do will be explained in the rest of this book. At this stage it is necessary to make just one point: we must *seek*. God has sought us. He is still seeking us. We must seek him. Indeed, God's chief quarrel with us is that we do not seek.

> The LORD looks down from heaven
>   on the human race
> to see if there are any who understand,
>   any who seek God.

All have turned away,
   all have become corrupt;
there is no-one who does good,
   not even one.[6]

Yet Jesus promised: 'Seek and you will find.' If we do not seek, we shall never find. Jesus told three stories to illustrate this point. The shepherd searched until he found the lost sheep. The woman hunted until she found her lost coin. The father was constantly on the lookout for his lost son. Why should we expect to do less? God desires to be found, but only by those who seek him.

We must seek *seriously*. 'Man is as lazy as he dares to be,' as the American writer Emerson put it. But what we're dealing with is so important that we must overcome our natural laziness and apathy and give our minds to the search. God has little patience with those who just trifle with him; 'he rewards those who earnestly seek him'.[7]

We must seek *humbly*. If apathy is a hindrance to some people, pride is an even greater and more common hindrance to others. We must freely admit that our minds, being finite, cannot possibly discover God by their own efforts. We depend on God to make himself known. I am not saying that we should suspend rational thinking. On the contrary, the psalmist encourages us *not* to be 'like the horse or the mule which have no understanding'. We must use our minds; but we must also admit their limitations. Jesus said, 'I praise you, Father, Lord of heaven and earth, because you have hidden these things from the wise and learned, and revealed them to little children.'

It is one of the reasons why Jesus loved children. They are teachable. They are not proud, self-important and critical. We need the open, humble and receptive mind of a little child.

We must seek *honestly*. We must come to what claims to be God's revelation of himself not only without pride, but without prejudice; not only with a humble mind, but with an open mind. All students know the dangers of approaching their subject with preconceived ideas. Yet many would-be enquirers come to the Bible with their minds already made up. We need to remember that God's promise is addressed only to the earnest seeker: 'You will seek me and find me when you seek me with all your heart.'[8] So we must lay aside our prejudice and open our minds to the possibility that Christianity may after all be true.

We must seek *obediently*. This is the hardest condition of all to fulfil. In seeking God we have to be prepared not only to revise our ideas, but to reform our lives. The Christian message has a moral challenge. If the message is true, this moral challenge has to be accepted. The point is that we cannot treat God as if he were an object for our detached scrutiny. We cannot fix him at the end of a telescope or a microscope and say, 'How interesting!' God is far from being merely interesting. He is deeply upsetting. The same is true of Jesus Christ.

> We had thought intellectually to examine him; we find he is spiritually examining us. The roles are reversed between us ... A person may study Jesus with intellectual impartiality, he cannot do it with moral neutrality ... We must declare our colours.[9]

This is what Jesus was getting at when, talking to some people in his own day who refused to accept him, he said, 'If anyone chooses to do God's will, he will find out whether my teaching comes from God or whether I speak on my own.' The promise is clear: we can certainly know whether Jesus Christ was true or false, whether his teaching was human or divine. But the promise has a moral condition attached to it. We have to be ready not just to believe, but to obey. We must be prepared to do God's will when he makes it known.

I remember a young man coming to see me when he had just left school and begun work in London. He had given up going to church, he said, because he could not say the creed without feeling that he was a hypocrite. He no longer believed it. When he had finished telling me what he thought, I said to him, 'If I were to answer your problems to your complete intellectual satisfaction, would you be willing to change the way you live?' He smiled slightly and blushed. The answer was clearly 'No'. His real problem was not intellectual but moral.

This, then, is the spirit in which our search must be conducted. We must set aside apathy, pride, prejudice and sin, and seek God – no matter what the consequences. Of all these hindrances to the search for truth, the last two are the hardest to overcome: intellectual prejudice and moral self-will. The reason is that both are expressions of fear – and fear is the greatest enemy of the truth. Fear paralyses our search. It isn't long before we realize that to find God and to accept Jesus Christ is a very inconvenient experience for most people. It would involve us rethinking our whole outlook on life and lead to major changes in the way we live. Such a combination of intellectual and moral cowardice makes us hesitate. We do not find because we do not seek. And the truth is that we do not seek because we do not really want to find. And the best way to be certain that we won't find is to decide against looking in the first place.

So let me urge you to be open to the possibility that you may not have got this right and that Christ may in fact be true. And if you want to be a humble, honest, obedient seeker after God,

spend some time reading the Bible, the book which claims to
be his revelation. Look particularly at the Gospels, which tell
the story of Jesus Christ. Give him the opportunity to confront
you with himself and to authenticate himself to you. Come
with the full consent of your mind and will, ready to believe
and obey if you become convinced that it's true. Why not
read through the Gospel of Mark, or John? You could read
either through in one go (preferably in a modern translation),
to let it make its total impact on you. Then you could reread it
slowly, say a chapter a day. Before you read, pray – perhaps
something along these lines:

> *God, if you exist (and I don't know you do), and you can hear this
> prayer (and I don't know if you can), I want to tell you that I am an
> honest seeker after the truth. Show me if Jesus is your Son and the
> Saviour of the world. And if you bring conviction to my mind, I will
> trust him as my Saviour and follow him as my Lord.*

No-one can pray such a prayer and be disappointed. God keeps
his promises. He honours all earnest searching. He rewards all
honest seekers. The undertaking given by Jesus is very clear:
'Seek and you will find.'

STUDY QUESTIONS

1. In what ways are the first four words of the Bible 'the key
   which opens our understanding to the Bible as a whole'?
2. How would you go about putting together 'a summary of
   the religion of the Bible'?
3. What differences are there between God's 'general' or
   'natural' revelation and his 'special' revelation? Why are
   these distinctions so important?

4. ' . . . it isn't enough for God simply to reveal himself to us in order to dispel our ignorance.' Why not? What more does he need to do?
5. What did Jesus come to do? In what ways does this make Christianity unique?
6. Why is it so important for us to 'seek' God? What does this mean in practice? How do we do it?

PART ONE:

WHO CHRIST IS

Chapter 2

THE CLAIMS
OF CHRIST

We have seen that we need to seek in order to find. But where are we to begin our search? The Christian answer is that we need to start with Jesus of Nazareth. The distinctively Christian claim about God is that he has spoken and acted fully and finally in Jesus Christ. So the crucial question is this: was this Jesus, the carpenter of Nazareth, the Son of God or not?

There are two main reasons why our investigation into Christianity should begin with the person of Christ. The first is that, in essence, Christianity *is* Christ. Who Christ is and what he has done are the rock upon which the Christian religion is built. If he was not who he said he was, and if he did not do what he said he had come to do, then the foundation is undermined and the whole thing will collapse. Take Christ from Christianity, and you remove the heart from it; there is practically nothing left. Christ is the centre of Christianity; everything else is peripheral. We are not concerned primarily with the effect he has had on the world, important though that is. Our concern is basically with the man himself. Who was he?

Secondly, once we accept that Jesus Christ is a uniquely divine person, many of the knots we get into with religion begin to untangle. For one thing, the divinity of Jesus helps us sort out questions about who God really is and what he is like. But it doesn't stop there. For if it's true that Jesus is divine, then it follows that what he taught must be true. And that sheds light on all sorts of important issues to do with Christian faith – such as (as we shall see) the purpose of life, what happens after death, the place of the Old Testament and the significance of the death of Jesus on the cross.

Take Christ from Christianity, and you remove the heart from it ... Christ is the centre of Christianity; everything else is peripheral.

Our investigation must therefore begin with Jesus Christ, and to study him properly we must turn to the Gospels in the New Testament. We don't need at this point to go along with the Christian view and accept them as the inspired Word of God. All we need to do is take them seriously as the undeniably historical documents that they are. This isn't the place to consider detailed questions about their literary origin.[1] It is sufficient just to emphasize that their authors were all Christians, that there's no reason to believe that Christians are any less honest than anyone else, and that what they say at least appears to be objective and to include the recollections of eyewitnesses. So for the time being, let me invite you to think of them simply as a substantially accurate record of the life and teaching of Jesus. In doing so, we're not going to rely on a few obscure and isolated proof texts. Instead we shall concentrate on what is clear and straightforward.

Our purpose is to bring together the main evidence which demonstrates that Jesus was the Son of God. It won't be enough to reach the conclusion that he simply exhibited a few divine characteristics. The truth to establish is his undeniable deity. Christians believe that Jesus has an eternal and essential relation to God that no-one else has or has ever had. We don't think of him as God in human disguise or as someone who simply displayed divine qualities to an impressive degree, but as the God-man. We are persuaded that Jesus was a historical person who possessed two distinct and perfect natures, one divine and one human, and that this makes him absolutely and for ever unique. In short, we believe him to be worthy not just of our admiration, but also of our worship.

The evidence is at least threefold. It concerns the claims he made, the character he displayed and his resurrection from the dead. No single argument is conclusive by itself. But these three strands weave together and point clearly to the same conclusion.

The first witness, then, is what Christ said about himself. In the words of Archbishop William Temple, 'It is now recognized that the one Christ for whose existence there is any evidence at all is a miraculous Figure making stupendous claims.' It is of course true that claims do not in themselves constitute evidence. But the claims that Jesus made are remarkable and demand some sort of an explanation. For the sake of clarity, we shall need to distinguish between four different kinds of claim.

HIS SELF-CENTRED TEACHING
The most striking feature of the teaching of Jesus is that he was constantly talking about himself. It is true that he said a great

deal about the fatherhood of God and the kingdom of God. But then he added that he is the Father's 'Son', and that he himself had come to launch the kingdom. Entry into the kingdom depends on how people respond to him personally. He even went so far as to call the kingdom of God 'my kingdom'.

This self-centredness of the teaching of Jesus immediately sets him apart from the other great religious teachers of the world. They tend to be self-effacing. He is self-advancing. They point people away from themselves, saying, 'That is the truth, so far as I understand it; follow that.' Jesus says, 'I am the truth; follow me.' No other religious founder who dared to say such a thing would be taken seriously. The personal pronoun forces itself repeatedly on our attention as we read his words. For example:

I am the bread of life. Whoever comes to me will never go hungry, and whoever believes in me will never be thirsty.

I am the light of the world. Whoever follows me will never walk in darkness, but will have the light of life.

I am the resurrection and the life. Anyone who believes in me will live, even though they die; and whoever lives by believing in me will never die.

I am the way and the truth and the life. No-one comes to the Father except through me.

Come to me, all you who are weary and burdened, and I will give you rest. Take my yoke upon you and learn from me... [2]

The great question to which the first phase of his teaching leads is, 'Who do you say that I am?' He refers back to figures from the distant past and makes the astonishing claim that Abraham rejoiced to see his day, that Moses wrote about him, that the Scriptures point to him, and that indeed in the three great divisions of the Old Testament – the Law, the Prophets and the Writings – there are things 'concerning himself'.[3]

Luke describes in some detail the dramatic visit which Jesus pays to the synagogue of his home village, Nazareth. He was given a scroll of the Old Testament Scriptures and he stood up to read. The passage is from the book of the prophet Isaiah 61:1–2:

> The Spirit of the Lord is on me,
>   because he has anointed me
>   to proclaim good news to the poor.
> He has sent me to proclaim freedom for the prisoners
>   and recovery of sight for the blind,
> to set the oppressed free,
>   to proclaim the year of the Lord's favour.[4]

He closed the book, returned it to the synagogue attendant and sat down, while the eyes of all the congregation were fastened on him. He then broke the silence with the amazing words, 'Today this scripture is fulfilled in your hearing.' In other words, 'Isaiah was writing about me.'

With such an opinion of himself, it comes as no surprise that he called people to himself. Indeed, he did more than offer a polite invitation; he issued a firm command. 'Come to me,' he said. 'Follow me.' If people would only come to him, he promised to lift the burdens of the weary, to satisfy the hungry, and to quench the longing of the thirsty soul.[5] More than that, his followers were to obey him and to make no secret of their allegiance to him. His disciples came to recognize the right of Jesus to make these wholesale claims, and in their letters Paul, Peter, James and Jude delight to describe themselves as his 'slaves'.

Furthermore, he offered himself to his contemporaries as someone in whom they should put their faith and to whom they should offer their love. People are supposed to believe in God – yet Jesus urged people to believe in himself. 'The work of God is this: to believe in the one he has sent.' 'Whoever believes in the Son has eternal life.' If to believe in him is our first duty, not to believe in him is our chief sin.[6]

Again, the first and greatest commandment is for us to love God with all that we are – heart and soul and mind. Yet Jesus audaciously claimed the supreme place for himself. Anyone who loves father, mother, son or daughter more than him is not worthy of him, he said. Indeed, resorting to the vivid Hebrew use of contrast to convey comparison, he added: 'If anyone comes to me and does not hate father and mother, wife and children, brothers and sisters – yes, even life itself – such a person cannot be my disciple.'[7]

So convinced was he of his central place in the purpose of God that he promised to send someone to take his place after he returned to heaven. This is the Holy Spirit. Christ's favourite name for him is translated in John's Gospel as the Advocate, the 'One who comes alongside to help'. It is a legal term, denoting a barrister, a counsel for the defence. It would be the Holy Spirit's task to carry forward the cause of Jesus. 'He will testify about me,' said Jesus. Again, 'He will glorify me because it is from me that he will receive what he will make known to you.'[8] So the Holy Spirit's role, both within the Christian community and in the wider world, would be to focus on Jesus Christ.

In one more flash of breathtaking egocentricity, Jesus predicted: 'I, when I am lifted up from the earth, will draw all people to myself.' He knew that the cross would be like a moral magnet which people would find most intriguing. But his understanding was that this attraction would bring them, first and foremost, not to God or the church, not to truth or to righteousness, but to himself. Indeed, it's only by being brought to him that people would come to embrace these other realities as well.

But the most remarkable feature of all this self-centred teaching is that it stemmed from one who insisted on humility in others. He rebuked his disciples for their self-seeking attitudes and was wearied by their desire to be great. But hold on a moment! Did he not practise what he preached? After all, he placed a little child before them and said that he was to be their model. Did he have a different standard for himself?

HIS DIRECT CLAIMS

Jesus clearly believed himself to be the Messiah predicted by the Old Testament. He came to establish what he called 'the kingdom of God', the coming of which had been foretold by generations of prophets.

It is significant that his first recorded words in the public arena were about the fulfilment of these ancient promises: 'The time has come; the kingdom of God has come near.' He assumed the title 'Son of Man', which is an accepted messianic title derived originally from one of the prophet Daniel's visions. He accepted the description 'Son of God' when challenged by the high priest at his trial, which is another messianic title taken particularly from Psalm 2:7. He also interpreted his mission in the light of the portrayal of the suffering servant of the Lord in the latter part of the book of

Isaiah. The first stage in his instruction of the core group of his disciples led up to an incident at Caesarea Philippi when Simon Peter declared his faith in Jesus as the Christ. Others might think of him as one of the prophets; but Simon has come to recognize him as the One to whom the prophets pointed. He is not just another signpost, but the destination to which the signposts have led.[9]

The whole account of what Jesus said and did is shaped by this sense of fulfilment. 'Blessed are the eyes that see what you see,' he once said privately to his disciples. 'For I tell you that many prophets and kings wanted to see what you see but did not see it, and to hear what you hear but did not hear it.'[10]

But the direct claims which concern us here refer not just to his being the Messiah, but to his deity. His claim to be the Son of God is more than messianic; it describes his unique and eternal relationship with God. Let's explore three examples of this greater claim.

First, there is the way he constantly referred to the close association he had with God as his 'Father'. Even as a boy of twelve he astonished his human parents with an uncompromising enthusiasm for his heavenly Father's business. And then he went on to say things like this:

> My Father is always at his work to this very day, and I, too, am working.

> I and the Father are one.

> I am in the Father and the Father is in me.[11]

It is true that he taught his disciples to address God as 'Father' as well, but the way in which he is the Son of God is so different from the way in which anyone else is a child of God that he has to distinguish between them. To him God is uniquely '*my* Father'. This is why, when talking with Mary Magdalene after his resurrection, he said, 'I am ascending to my Father and your Father.' It just wouldn't have been appropriate for him to say, 'I ascend to *our* Father.'

These verses are all taken from John's Gospel, but the same unique relationship with God is claimed by Jesus in Matthew 11:27 where he says, 'All things have been committed to me by my Father. No-one knows the Son except the Father, and no-one knows the Father except the Son and those to whom the Son chooses to reveal him.'

That Jesus did in fact claim this very close relationship with God is further confirmed by the indignation which he aroused in the religious leaders who opposed him. He 'claimed to be the Son of God', they said.[12] His identification with God was so close that it was natural for him to equate the attitude people had to him with the attitude they had to God. In short:

to know him is to know God;
to see him is to see God;
to believe in him is to believe in God;
to receive him is to receive God;
to hate him is to hate God;
to honour him is to honour God.[13]

These are some of the general claims which Jesus made about his unique relationship to God. He also made two more direct claims. The first is recorded at the end of the eighth chapter of John's Gospel. In an argument with some of the Jewish leaders he said: 'Very truly I tell you, whoever obeys my word will never see death' (TNIV). This was too much for his critics.

'Abraham died', they expostulated, 'and so did the prophets . . .
Are you greater than our father Abraham? . . . Who do you
think you are?'

'Your father Abraham rejoiced at the thought of seeing my
day,' Jesus replied.

They were yet more puzzled. 'You are not yet fifty years old
. . . and you have seen Abraham!'

And Jesus responded with one of the most far-reaching
claims he ever made: 'Very truly I tell you . . . before Abraham
was born, I am!' (TNIV)

Then they picked up stones to throw at him.

According to the law of Moses, stoning was the penalty for
blasphemy. At first sight, we might wonder what they saw as
blasphemous in what Jesus said. Of course there is the claim to
have lived before Abraham. This was a claim he often made.
He had 'come down' from heaven and 'been sent' by the
Father, for example. But this claim was innocent enough. We
must look further. The clue comes from the fact that he didn't
say 'Before Abraham was, I *was*', but 'Before Abraham was,
I *am*'. Jesus was claiming that he had existed eternally before
Abraham. But even that is not all. For 'I am' implies a claim
not only to eternity, but also to deity. 'I am' is the divine Name
by which God had revealed himself to Moses, when he was
travelling through the desert and encountered God at the
burning bush. 'I AM WHO I AM. This is what you are to say to
the Israelites: "I AM has sent me to you." ' It is this divine title
that Jesus quietly used of himself. This is what led the religious
leaders to pick up stones in order to punish what they saw as
the blasphemy of Jesus.

The second example of a direct claim to deity took place
after the resurrection (assuming for the moment that the
resurrection took place). John reports (20:26–29) that on

the Sunday following Easter Day, doubting Thomas (who had missed the appearance of Jesus a week earlier) was with the other disciples in the upper room when Jesus appeared. He invited Thomas to touch his wounds, and Thomas, over-whelmed with wonder, cried out, 'My Lord and my God!' Jesus calmly accepted this description of himself. He rebuked Thomas, yes – but for his unbelief, not for his worship.

HIS INDIRECT CLAIMS

It isn't only the things which Jesus said directly that support his claim to deity. There are also the indirect ways in which he made it clear that this is how he saw himself. The implications of what he was doing were as eloquent an indication of who he is as were his plain statements. On many occasions he did things which only God should do. We'll look at four of them.

The first is the claim to *forgive sins*. On two separate occasions,[14] Jesus is recorded as forgiving sinners. The first time, the friends of a paralysed man brought him to Jesus by letting him down through the roof on the mat he was using as a bed. Jesus recognized that his need was basically spiritual and surprised the crowd by saying to him, 'Son, your sins are forgiven,' before going on to heal his physical problem as well.

The second declaration of forgiveness was made to a woman known to be living an immoral life, who came to see Jesus while he was having a meal at the home of a religious leader. She came up behind him while he was reclining at the table and washed his feet with her tears. Then she wiped them with her hair, kissed them and poured perfume on them. And Jesus said to her, 'Your sins are forgiven.'

On both occasions the onlookers raise their eyebrows and ask, 'Who is this? What blasphemy is this? Who but God can forgive sins?' They're quite right to be concerned. We may forgive the injuries which others do to us; but the sins we commit against God can surely only be forgiven by God himself.

Christ's second indirect claim is to *give life*. He described himself as 'the bread of life', 'the life' and 'the resurrection and the life'. He likened his followers' dependence on him to the sustenance derived from the vine by its branches. He offered a woman from Samaria 'living water' and promised eternal life to a rich young man if he will come and follow him. He called himself the Good Shepherd who will not only give his life for the sheep, but give life to them. He stated that God has granted him authority over all people that he might give life to as many as God gives him, and declared, 'The Son gives life to whom he is pleased to give it.'[15]

So definite is this claim that his disciples clearly recognized the truth of it. It made leaving him impossible. 'To whom shall we go?' asked Peter. 'You have the words of eternal life.'

Life is an enigma. Whether we're talking about physical life or spiritual life, its nature is as baffling as its origin. We can neither define what it is, nor state where it comes from. We can only call it a gift from God. It is this gift which Jesus claims to give.

Christ's third indirect claim is to *teach the truth*. It is not so much the truths which he taught as the direct and dogmatic manner in which he taught them which attracts our attention. His contemporaries were deeply impressed by his wisdom.

Where did this man get these things? ... What's this wisdom that has been given to him? ... Isn't this the carpenter?

How did this man get such learning without having been taught?

But they were even more impressed by his authority.

No-one ever spoke the way this man does.

His words had authority.

When Jesus had finished saying these things, the crowds were amazed at his teaching, because he taught as one who had authority, and not as their teachers of the law.[16]

His authority was unlike that of the experts in religious law, who never taught without quoting from the authorities which backed them up. Neither was it like the authority of the prophets. They spoke with the authority of God, but Jesus claimed an authority all of his own. His formula was not 'This is what *God* says', but 'This is what *I* say'. It is true that he said that his ideas were not his own, but came from the Father who sent him. Even so, he knew himself to be such a clear source of divine revelation that he was able to speak with enormous personal confidence. He never hesitated or apologized. He had no need to contradict, withdraw or modify anything he said. He spoke the unequivocal words of God: 'He whom God has sent utters the words of God.' He predicted the future with complete conviction. He issued absolute moral commands like 'Love your enemies', 'Do not worry about your life', 'Do not judge, or you too will be judged'. He made promises with no doubt that they would be honoured: 'Ask and it will be given to you.' He asserted that, even though heaven and earth pass away, his words will never go the same way. He warned those who heard him that their destiny depended on how they chose to respond to his teaching – just as, in Old Testament times, the destiny of the people of Israel had depended on their response to God's Word.

Christ's fourth indirect claim is to *judge the world*. This is perhaps the most extraordinary of all his statements. Several of his parables imply that he personally will come back at the end of the world, and that the final day of reckoning will not take place until then. He will himself wake up the dead, and the whole world will be gathered before him. He will sit on the throne of his glory, and the judgment will be entrusted to him by the Father. He will then separate people from one another as a shepherd separates his sheep from his goats. Some will be invited to come and inherit the kingdom prepared for them since the creation of the world. Others will hear the dreadful words, 'Depart from me, you who are cursed, into the eternal fire prepared for the devil and his angels.'[17]

Not only will Jesus be the Judge, but the basis of judgment will be people's attitude to him as shown in their treatment of his 'brothers and sisters' or their response to his word. He will acknowledge before his Father in heaven those who have publicly acknowledged him; he will disown those who have publicly disowned him. Indeed, to be excluded from heaven on the last day, it will be enough for Jesus to say to them, quite simply, 'I never knew you.'[18]

It is hard to exaggerate the enormity of this claim. Imagine a minister addressing his congregation in these terms today: 'Listen carefully to my words. Your eternal destiny depends on it. I am going to return at the end of the world to judge you, and your fate will be settled according to whether or not you obey me.' Such a preacher would soon be under psychiatric care!

HIS DRAMATIZED CLAIMS

It remains for us to consider the recorded miracles of Jesus. A helpful way of approaching these is to see them as his dramatized claims.

This is no place for a thorough discussion of whether or not miracles can happen or what they are for. All we need do here is to make the point that the value of Christ's miracles comes not so much from their supernatural character as from their spiritual significance. They were 'signs' as well as 'wonders'. They were never performed selfishly or senselessly. Their purpose was not to show off or to force people into submission. They were not so much demonstrations of special power as illustrations of moral authority. They are in fact the acted parables of Jesus. They demonstrate his claims visually. The things he does dramatize the things he says.

John understood this very clearly. He constructs his Gospel around six or seven selected 'signs' (see 20:30–31), and associates them with the great 'I am' declarations which Jesus made in his preaching and teaching. The first sign was the changing of water into wine at a wedding reception in Cana of Galilee. The event itself doesn't really tell us very much. Its significance lies more beneath the surface. John tells us that the stone water jars stood ready 'for ceremonial washing'. What we might pass over as merely an incidental reference turns out to be the clue we are seeking. The water stood for the old religion. The wine stood for the religion of Jesus. Just as he changed the water into wine, so his gospel would supersede the law. The sign backed up the claim that Jesus was the one who would bring in this new order. He was the Messiah. As he was soon to say to the Samaritan woman, 'I am he.'

Similarly, his feeding of the five thousand illustrated his claim to satisfy the hunger of the human heart. 'I am the bread of life,' he said. A little later, he opened the eyes of a man born blind, having earlier stated, 'I am the light of the world.' If he could restore sight to the blind, he can open people's eyes to see and to know God. Finally, he brought back to life a man called Lazarus who had been dead for four days, and claimed, 'I am the resurrection and the life.' He had resuscitated a dead man. Again, it was a sign. The life of the body symbolizes the life of the soul. Christ could be the life of the believer before death and will be the resurrection of the believer after death. All these miracles are parables, illustrating the truth that as human beings we are spiritually hungry, blind and dead, and that only Christ can satisfy our hunger, restore our sight and raise us to a new life.[19]

CONCLUSION

It just isn't possible to eliminate these claims from the teaching of the carpenter of Nazareth. We can't say that they were invented by the evangelists, nor even that they were unconsciously exaggerated. They are widely and evenly distributed in the different Gospels and sources of the Gospels, and the portrait is too consistent and too balanced to have been dreamed up by the writers.

The claims are there. It is of course true that they do not in themselves constitute evidence of deity. After all, claims can be false. But some explanation of them must be found. We simply can't go on treating Jesus as a great teacher if he was completely mistaken in one of the chief subjects of his teaching – himself. As many scholars have recognized, there is a certain disturbing 'megalomania' about Jesus.

These claims in a mere man would be egoism carried even to imperial megalomania.[20]

The discrepancy between the depth and sanity, and (let me add) *shrewdness*, of his moral teaching and the rampant megalomania which must lie behind his theological teaching unless he is indeed God, has never been satisfactorily got over.[21]

Was he then a deliberate impostor? Did he attempt to persuade people to accept his views by assuming a divine authority he did not possess? This is very difficult to believe. Jesus comes across as being entirely straightforward in his dealings with people. He hated hypocrisy in others and was transparently sincere himself.

Was he then sincerely mistaken? Did he have a fixed delusion about himself? This possibility has its supporters, but leaves one feeling that their delusion is greater than his. Jesus does not give the impression of the sort of abnormality which one expects to find in those who are deluded. His claims appear to be supported by his character, which is what we shall look at next.

STUDY QUESTIONS

1. Why should an investigation into Christianity begin with the person of Jesus Christ?
2. How would you justify the use of the Gospels as reliable sources of information about Jesus?
3. What are the three main strands of evidence which lead to the conclusion that Jesus is 'worthy not just of our admiration, but also of our worship'?
4. What is so remarkable about the self-centredness of Jesus' teaching?
5. In what ways did Jesus claim, both directly and indirectly, to be the Son of God?
6. Why would it be wrong simply to label Jesus as a 'great teacher'?

Chapter 3

THE CHARACTER
OF CHRIST

Some years ago I received a letter from a young man I knew slightly. 'I have just made a great discovery,' he wrote. 'Almighty God had two sons. Jesus Christ was the first; I am the second.' I glanced at the address at the top of his letter. He was writing from a well-known psychiatric hospital.

There have of course been many pretenders to greatness and to divinity. Psychiatric hospitals are full of deluded people who claim to be Julius Caesar, the prime minister, the president of the United States or Jesus Christ. But no-one believes them. No-one is deceived except themselves. They have no disciples, except perhaps their fellow patients. They fail to convince other people for the simple reason that they don't actually seem to be what they claim to be. Their claims are not supported by their character.

Now the Christian's conviction about Christ is greatly strengthened by the fact that he really does appear to be who he said he was. There is no inconsistency between his words and his deeds. There is no doubt that he would need to be a

very remarkable character in order to authenticate his extravagant claims. But Christians believe that he was exactly that. His
character doesn't prove his claims to be true, but it does
strongly confirm them. His claims were exclusive. His character was unique. Carnegie Simpson wrote:

> Instinctively we do not class him with others . . . Jesus is not one of
> the group of the world's great. Talk about Alexander the Great
> and Charles the Great and Napoleon the Great if you will . . . Jesus
> is apart. He is not the Great; he is the Only. He is simply
> Jesus. Nothing could add to that.[1]

Napoleon himself wrote:

> Alexander, Caesar, Charlemagne, and I have founded empires.
> But on what did we rest the creations of our genius? Upon force.
> Jesus Christ founded his empire upon love . . .

But even to say that Jesus is 'the greatest man who has ever
lived' doesn't fully do him justice. The point is that when it
comes to thinking about where he stands in relation to other
dominant figures from history, we're not comparing like with
like. We need to focus instead on the complete contrast that
there is between him and everyone else. 'Why do you call me
good?' he asked someone on one occasion. 'No-one is good –
except God alone.' That's it exactly. It's not simply that he is
better than others, nor even that he is the best human being
who has ever lived, but that he is good – good with the absolute
goodness of God.

The importance of this claim is very clear. What Christians
call sin is a congenital disease which is endemic throughout the
human race. We are all born with its infection in our nature. It

is a universal ailment. Therefore, if the claim that Jesus of Nazareth was without sin is true, then he cannot have been human in exactly the same way that the rest of us are human. If he really was sinless, he was distinct from us. He was supernatural.

His character was more wonderful than the greatest miracle.[2]

This separateness from sinners is not a little, but a stupendous thing; it is the presupposition of redemption; it is that very virtue in Christ without which he would not be qualified to be a Saviour, but would, like us, need to be saved.[3]

We can summarize the evidence for the sinlessness of Christ under four headings.

WHAT CHRIST HIMSELF THOUGHT

On one or two occasions Jesus stated directly that he was without sin. When a woman was discovered in the act of adultery and dragged before him, he issued an embarrassing challenge to her accusers, 'Let any one of you who is without sin be the first to throw a stone at her' (TNIV). Gradually they drifted away until there was no-one left. A little later in the same chapter (John 8), it is recorded that Jesus issued another challenge, this time about himself: 'Can any of you prove me guilty of sin?' No-one could answer. They slipped away when he accused them. But when the roles were reversed and he invited them to accuse him, he had no difficulty at all in staying where he was and bearing their scrutiny. They were all sinners; he was without sin. He lived a life of perfect obedience to his Father's will. 'I always do what pleases him,' he said. There was nothing boastful about those words. He spoke entirely natur-ally, with no fuss or pretension.

Similarly, by the very nature of his teaching, he placed himself in a moral category all by himself. One of his stories was about two men who went to the temple to pray. The first, a Pharisee, came up with a prayer of arrogant thanksgiving, 'God, I thank you that I am not like other people.' But you wouldn't ever find Jesus himself doing anything like that. His uniqueness was completely unselfconscious. He didn't need to draw attention to it. It was a fact so obvious to him that it didn't need emphasizing. It was implied rather than asserted. Everyone else was a lost sheep; he had come as the Good Shepherd to seek and to save them. Everyone else was sick with the disease of sin; he was the doctor who had come to heal them. Everyone else was trapped in the darkness of sin and ignorance; he was the light of the world. Everyone else was a sinner; he was born to be their Saviour and would die for the forgiveness of their sins. Everyone else was hungry; he was the bread of life. Everyone else was dead in wrongdoing and sin; he could be their life now and their resurrection in the future. All these metaphors express the moral uniqueness of which he was clearly conscious.

It is not surprising, therefore, that although we are told about the temptations of Jesus, we hear nothing of his sins. He never confesses his sins or asks for forgiveness, although he tells his disciples to do so. He shows no awareness at all of moral failure. He appears to have no feeling of guilt and no sense of separation from God. He did indeed go through John the Baptist's 'baptism of repentance'. But John tried to discourage Jesus from being baptized, and Jesus submitted to it, not because he needed to admit to being a sinner, but so that he could 'fulfil all righteousness' and begin to identify himself with the sins of others. He himself seems to have lived in unbroken communion with his Father.

This absence of all moral discontent and sense of unclouded friendship with God are particularly remarkable for two reasons. The first is that Jesus possessed a keen moral judgment. He did not need to be told what other human beings were like because 'he knew what was in them'. The Gospel accounts often record his ability to read the inner questions and perplexities of the crowd. His clear perception led him fearlessly to expose the duplicity of the religious leaders. He hated their hypocrisy. He pronounced woes upon them as thunderous as those of the Old Testament prophets. Ostentation and pretence disgusted him. Yet his penetrating eye saw no sin in himself.

The second reason why his self-conscious purity is astonishing is that it is quite unlike the experience of other holy people. Christians know that the closer they get to God, the more they become aware of their own sin. In this the saint is rather like the scientist. The more scientists find out, the more they realize how little they know and how much there is still to discover. Similarly, the more Christians grow in their imitation of Christ, the more aware they become of the vast distance which still separates them from him.

A glance into any Christian biography underlines this – if our own experience is not sufficient evidence. Let me offer just one example. David Brainerd was a young pioneer missionary among the Indians of Delaware at the beginning of the nineteenth century. His diary and letters reveal the rich quality of his devotion to Christ. Despite great pain and crippling weakness, which led to his death at the age of twenty-nine, he gave himself totally to his work. He travelled on horseback through thick forests, preached and taught without rest, slept out in the open, and was content to have no settled home or family life. His diary is full of expressions of love to 'my dear Indians' and of prayers and praises to his Saviour.

We might imagine that he is a saint of the first order. Surely his life and work can't have been unduly tainted by sin. Yet as we turn the pages of his diary, he continually laments what he describes as his moral 'corruption'. He complains of his lack of prayer and the poverty of his love for Christ. He calls himself 'a poor worm', 'a dead dog', and 'an unspeakably worthless wretch'. This is not because he had a morbid conscience. It was the closeness of his relationship with Christ that made him so painfully aware of his sinfulness.

Jesus Christ, who lived more closely to God than anybody else has done, was free from all sense of sin.

Yet Jesus Christ, who lived more closely to God than anybody else has done, was free from all sense of sin.

WHAT CHRIST'S FRIENDS SAID

It is clear, then, that Jesus believed himself to be sinless, just as he believed himself to be the Messiah and the Son of God. But could he have got this all wrong? One way of approaching this is to ask what others thought at the time. Did his disciples share the extraordinary opinion he had of himself?

We may feel that the disciples of Christ were not particularly good witnesses. It has been argued that they were biased, and that they deliberately painted him in rather more glowing colours than he deserved. But this is very unfair. Their statements cannot be dismissed so lightly. There are several reasons why we can be confident in what they say about him.

First, they were in close contact with Jesus for about three years. They lived together. They experienced the cramped conditions of the same boat. They even had a common purse (and a common bank account can be a potent cause of discord!). The disciples got on one another's nerves. They quarrelled. But they never found in Jesus the sins they found in themselves. Familiarity normally breeds contempt, but not in this case. Indeed, two of the chief witnesses to the sinlessness of Christ are Peter and John (as we shall see later), and they belonged to that inner group (consisting of Peter, James and John) to whom he gave special privileges and particular opportunities to get to know him better.

Secondly, what the apostles say about this can be trusted because they were Jews whose minds had been soaked since childhood in the teaching of the Old Testament. And one Old Testament doctrine which they had certainly taken on board is the universal character of human sin:

> All have turned away,
>   all have become corrupt;
> there is no-one who does good,
>   not even one.
> (TNIV)

> We all, like sheep, have gone astray,
>   each of us has turned to our own way.
> (TNIV)

In the light of this teaching from the Bible, the idea that someone could be without sin is not one which they would have been able to accept at all easily.

Thirdly, the testimony of the apostles to the sinlessness of Jesus is all the more credible because it is indirect. They do not set out to establish the truth that he was without sin. Their references to this are asides. They are discussing some other subject, and refer to his being without sin almost as an afterthought.

This is what they say. Peter first describes Jesus as 'a lamb without blemish or defect' and then says that he 'committed no sin, and no deceit was found in his mouth'. John roundly declares that every human being is a sinner, and that if we say we have no sin or have not sinned, we both are liars ourselves and make God a liar too. But then he goes on to say that in Christ, who came to take away our sins, there 'is no sin'.[4]

To what Peter and John tell us we can add the words of Paul and of the author of the New Testament letter to the Hebrews. They describe Jesus as one who 'had no sin', but rather was 'holy, blameless, pure, set apart from sinners'. He was indeed 'tempted in every way, just as we are – yet he did not sin'.[5]

WHAT CHRIST'S ENEMIES CONCEDED

We may consider ourselves to be on safer ground when we come to look at what the enemies of Jesus thought of him. They certainly had no bias – at least not in his favour. We read in the Gospels that 'they watched him closely' and tried to 'trap him in his words'. It is well known that when a debate cannot be won by reasoning, then people all too readily descend to personal abuse. If arguments are lacking, mud is a good substitute. Even the history of the church is sadly smudged by the dirt of personal attacks. So it was with the enemies of Jesus.

The Gospel writer Mark sets out four of their criticisms (in 2:1 – 3:6). Their first accusation was *blasphemy*. Jesus had forgiven a man's sins. This was a clear invasion of divine territory. It was blasphemous arrogance, they said. But this is to beg the question. If he were indeed divine, it was entirely appropriate for him to forgive sins.

Next, they were (they said) horrified by *his evil associations*. He spent time with bad people. He ate with those who were on the margins of society. He allowed prostitutes to approach him. No Pharisee would dream of behaving like this. He would gather his robes around him and recoil from contact with such scum. He would have thought himself entirely right to do so, too. He would not appreciate the grace and tenderness of Jesus who, though 'set apart from sinners', yet earned the honoured title 'friend of sinners'.

Their third accusation was that *his religion was frivolous*. He did not fast and go without food like the Pharisees, or even like the disciples of John the Baptist. He was 'a glutton and a drunkard' who came 'eating and drinking'. Such an attack hardly deserves a serious refutation. It's true that Jesus was full of joy, but there can be no doubt that he took religion seriously.

Fourth, they were incensed by *his sabbath-breaking*. He healed sick people on the Sabbath day, the one day in the week when people weren't supposed to do any work. And his disciples even walked through the cornfields on the Sabbath, picking and eating corn, something which the teachers of the law and Pharisees forbade as practically the same as the farmer's labour of reaping and threshing. Yet no-one can doubt that Jesus submitted to God's law. He obeyed it himself, and in debate would refer his opponents to it as the ultimate source of authority. He also affirmed that God had made the Sabbath, and that he had done so for the benefit of humanity. But being himself 'Lord of the Sabbath', he claimed the right to set aside erroneous human traditions and to give God's law its true interpretation.

All these accusations are either trivial or question-begging. So when Jesus was on trial for his life, his detractors had to hire false witnesses against him. But even then they were unable to agree with one another. In fact, the only charge they could come up with was not moral but political. Time after time, his court appearances made it clear that he was blameless. The Roman governor Pontius Pilate, after several cowardly attempts to evade the issue, publicly washed his hands and declared himself 'innocent of this man's blood'. King Herod could find no fault in him either. Judas the traitor, filled with remorse, returned the thirty pieces of silver to the priests with the words, 'I have sinned, for I have betrayed innocent blood.' The penitent thief on the cross rebuked his fellow criminal for having a go at Jesus and added, 'This man has done nothing wrong.' Finally, the centurion, having watched Jesus suffer and die, exclaimed, 'Surely this was a righteous man.'[6]

WHAT WE CAN SEE FOR OURSELVES

In assessing the character of Jesus Christ, we do not need to rely only on the testimony of others; we can make our own estimate. The moral perfection which was quietly claimed by him, confidently asserted by his friends and reluctantly acknowledged by his enemies, is clearly shown in the Gospels.

We are given plenty of opportunity to form our own judgment. The picture of Jesus painted by the four evangelists, Matthew, Mark, Luke and John, is a comprehensive one. It's true that it depicts largely his public ministry of barely three years. But we are given a glimpse of his boyhood, and Luke twice repeats that during his hidden years at Nazareth he was developing naturally in body, mind and spirit, and was growing in favour with God and people.

We see him spending time in private with his disciples, and we watch him in the noisy bustle of the crowd. He is brought before us in the work he did in Galilee, facing the pressures of being hero-worshipped by the mob who wanted to take him by force and make him a king. And we're able to follow him into the cloisters of the Jerusalem temple where Pharisees and Sadducees were united against him in their subtle inquisition. But whether scaling the dizzy heights of success or plunged into the lonely depths of bitter rejection, he is the same Jesus. He is consistent. He has no moods. He does not change.

Again, the portrait is balanced. There is no trace of the crank in him. He believes ardently in what he teaches, but he is not a fanatic. Some of what he has to say is unpopular, but he is not eccentric. There is as much evidence for his humanity as for his divinity. He gets tired. He needs to sleep and eat and drink like other people. He experiences the human emotions of love and anger, joy and sorrow. He is fully human. Yet he is no mere man.

Above all, he is unselfish. Perhaps nothing strikes us more than this. Although he clearly believed himself to be divine, he did not put on airs or stand on his dignity. He was never pompous. There was no touch of self-importance about Jesus. He was humble.

It is this paradox which is so amazing, this combination of the self-centredness of his teaching and the unself-centredness of his behaviour. In thought he put himself first; in deed last. He exhibited both the greatest self-esteem and the greatest self-sacrifice. He knew himself to be the Lord of all, but he became their servant. He said that he would one day come to judge the world, but he washed the feet of his friends.

Never has anyone given up so much. It is claimed (by him as well as by those who tell us about him) that he renounced the joys of heaven for the sorrows of earth, exchanging an eternal immunity to the approach of sin for painful contact with evil in this world. He was born of a lowly Hebrew mother in a dirty stable in the insignificant village of Bethlehem. He became a refugee baby in Egypt. He was brought up in the obscure hamlet of Nazareth, and toiled at a carpenter's bench to support his mother and the other children in their home. Eventually he became a travelling preacher, with few possessions, small comforts and no home. He made friends with ordinary people. He touched those with leprosy and allowed prostitutes to touch him. He gave himself away in a ministry of healing, helping, teaching and preaching.

He was misunderstood and misrepresented, and became the victim of people's prejudices and vested interests. He was despised and rejected by his own people, and deserted by his friends. He gave his back to be flogged, his face to be spat upon, his head to be crowned with thorns, his hands and feet to be nailed to a common Roman gallows. And, as the cruel spikes were driven home, he kept praying for his tormentors, 'Father, forgive them, for they do not know what they are doing.'

Such a man is altogether beyond our reach. He succeeded where we always fail. He had complete self-mastery. He never retaliated. He never grew resentful or irritable. He had such control of himself that, whatever others might think or say or do, he would deny himself and abandon himself to the will of God and the welfare of his fellow human beings. 'I seek not to please myself,' he said, and 'I am not seeking glory for myself.' As Paul wrote, 'For Christ did not please himself.'

This utter disregard of self in the service of God and man is what the Bible calls love. There is no self-interest in love. The essence of love is self-sacrifice. Even the worst of us is adorned by an occasional flash of such nobility, but the life of Jesus radiated it with a never-fading incandescent glow.

Jesus was sinless because he was selfless. Such selflessness is love. And God is love.

STUDY QUESTIONS

1. Why is it that even to describe Jesus as 'the greatest man who has ever lived' doesn't fully do him justice?
2. How do we know that Jesus considered himself to be without sin?
3. Were the disciples of Jesus biased? Why should we take what they say about his character seriously?
4. What failings did the enemies of Jesus identify in him? Were they right?
5. What strikes you about what the Gospels reveal of the character of Jesus?
6. What is the paradox that surfaces when we set the claims of Christ alongside his character?

Chapter 4

THE RESURRECTION OF CHRIST

We have considered the extravagant claims which Jesus made and the selfless character which he displayed. We now come to examine the evidence for his historical resurrection from the dead.

Clearly, if it is true, the resurrection is enormously significant. If Jesus of Nazareth rose from the dead, then he was beyond dispute a unique figure. It is not a question of his spiritual survival, nor of his physical resuscitation, but of his conquest of death and his resurrection to a new plane of existence altogether. We do not know of anyone else who has had this experience. Modern people are therefore as scornful as the philosophers in Athens who heard Paul preach on the Areopagus: 'When they heard about the resurrection of the dead, some of them sneered.'

The argument is not that his resurrection establishes his deity, but that it fits with it. It is only to be expected that a supernatural person would come to and leave the earth in a supernatural way. This is in fact what the New Testament

teaches and what, because of this, the church has always
believed. His birth was natural, but his conception was supernatural. His death was natural, but his resurrection was
supernatural. His miraculous conception and resurrection do
not prove his deity, but they are consistent with it.[1]

Jesus himself never predicted his death without adding that
he would rise, and described his coming resurrection as a 'sign'.
Paul, at the beginning of his letter to the Romans, wrote that
Jesus was 'appointed the Son of God in power by his
resurrection from the dead' (TNIV), and the earliest sermons
of the apostles recorded in the Acts repeatedly assert that it was
through the resurrection that God reversed the human court's
verdict on Jesus and completely vindicated him.

In writing about the resurrection, Luke, who is known to
have been a painstaking and accurate historian, says that there
are 'many convincing proofs'. We may not feel able to go as far
as Thomas Arnold, who called the resurrection 'the best attested
fact in history', but certainly many impartial investigators have
judged the evidence to be extremely good. For instance, Sir
Edward Clarke KC wrote to the Rev. E. L. Macassey:

> As a lawyer I have made a prolonged study of the evidences for the
> events of the first Easter Day. To me the evidence is conclusive,
> and over and over again in the High Court I have secured the
> verdict on evidence not nearly so compelling. Inference follows on
> evidence, and a truthful witness is always artless and disdains
> effect. The Gospel evidence for the resurrection is of this class, and
> as a lawyer I accept it unreservedly as the testimony of truthful
> men to facts they were able to substantiate.

What is this evidence? It can be summarized by making four
statements.

THE BODY HAD GONE

The resurrection accounts in the four Gospels begin with the visit of certain women to the tomb early on Easter Sunday morning. When they arrived they were stunned to discover that the body of Jesus had disappeared.

A few weeks later the apostles began to preach that Jesus had risen. It was the main thrust of their message. But they could hardly have expected anyone to believe them if the body of Jesus was still in Joseph's tomb – just a few minutes' walk away! No. The tomb was empty. The body had gone. There can be no doubt about this fact. The question is how to explain it.

First, there is the theory that *the women went to the wrong tomb*. It was still dark, and they were overwhelmed with sorrow. The claim is that they could easily have made a mistake.

This sounds plausible on the surface, but it doesn't stand up. To begin with, it cannot have been completely dark. It is true that John says the women came 'while it was still dark'. But in Matthew 28:1 it is 'at dawn', while Luke says it was 'very early in the morning', and Mark distinctly states that it was 'just after sunrise'.

Furthermore, these women weren't fools. At least two of them had seen for themselves where Joseph and Nicodemus had laid the body. They had even watched the whole process of burial, 'sitting there opposite the tomb'. The same two (Mary Magdalene and Mary the mother of Joses) returned at dawn, bringing with them Salome, Joanna and 'the other women', so that if one mistook the path or the tomb, she is likely to have been corrected by the others. And if Mary Magdalene went to the wrong place the first time, she can hardly have repeated her error when she returned in the full light of morning and stayed on in the garden till Jesus met her.

Besides, it wasn't mere sentiment that brought them to the tomb so early in the morning. They had a job to do. They had bought spices and were going to complete the anointing of their Lord's body, since the timing of the burial so close to the Sabbath had meant that they couldn't complete the task properly two days previously. These devoted and businesslike women were not the kind to be easily deceived or to give up on what they had come to do. Again, even if *they* mistook the tomb, would Peter and John, who ran to verify their story, make the same mistake, and others who doubtless came later, including Joseph and Nicodemus themselves?

The second explanation of the empty tomb is *the coma theory*. Those who uphold this view maintain that Jesus did not actually die on the cross, but only lost consciousness. He then revived in the tomb, left it and later made himself known to the disciples.

This theory simply bristles with problems. It is thoroughly perverse. The evidence entirely contradicts it. Pilate was indeed surprised that Jesus was already dead, but he was sufficiently convinced by the centurion's assurance to give Joseph permission to remove the body from the cross. The reason the centurion was so certain is that he must have been present when 'one of the soldiers pierced Jesus' side with a spear, bringing a sudden flow of blood and water'. So Joseph and Nicodemus took down his body, wrapped it in strips of linen and laid it in Joseph's new tomb.

Are we then seriously to believe that Jesus had just temporarily lost consciousness? That after the rigours and pains of trial, mockery, flogging and crucifixion he could survive thirty-six hours in a stone tomb with neither warmth nor food nor medical care? That he could then rally sufficiently to perform the superhuman feat of shifting the boulder which was in front of the mouth of the tomb, and this without disturbing the Roman guard? That then, weak and sickly and hungry, he could appear to the disciples in such a way as to give them the impression that he had vanquished death? That he could go on to claim that he had died and risen, could send them out all over the world and promise to be with them to the end of time? That he could live somewhere in hiding for forty days, making occasional surprise appearances, and then finally disappear without any explanation? Such a view is incredible.

Thirdly, there is the idea that *thieves stole the body*. There is no shred of evidence for this supposition. Nor is it explained how thieves could have fooled the Roman guard. Nor can one imagine why thieves should have taken the body, but left the strips of linen it was wrapped in, nor what possible motive they could have had for doing such a thing.

Fourthly, it has been argued that the *disciples removed the body*. This, Matthew tells us, is the rumour which the Jewish authorities spread right from the start. He describes how Pilate, having given permission to Joseph to remove Christ's body, received a deputation of chief priests and Pharisees, who said:

> Sir, we remember that while he was still alive that deceiver said, 'After three days I will rise again.' So give the order for the tomb to be made secure until the third day. Otherwise, his disciples may come and steal the body and tell the people that he has been raised from the dead. This last deception will be worse than the first.

Pilate agreed. 'Go, make the tomb as secure as you know how,' he said, and so they 'made the tomb secure by putting a seal on the stone and posting the guard'. Matthew goes on to describe how the stone, the seal and the guard could not prevent the resurrection, and how the guard went into the city to report to the chief priests what had happened. After consultation they bribed the soldiers and told them:

> You are to say, 'His disciples came during the night and stole him away while we were asleep.' If this report gets to the governor, we will satisfy him and keep you out of trouble. So the soldiers took the money and did as they were instructed. And this story has been widely circulated among the Jews to this very day.

But the story does not hold water. Is it likely that a highly disciplined detachment of guards, whether Roman or Jewish, would all fall asleep on duty? And if any of them stayed awake, how did the women get past them and roll back the stone?

Even supposing the disciples could have succeeded in removing the body of Jesus, there is a significant psychological consideration which is enough to pour cold water on the whole theory. We learn from the first part of the Acts of the Apostles that the resurrection was what they concentrated on in their early preaching. 'You killed him, but God raised him, and we are witnesses,' they kept saying. Are we then to believe that they were proclaiming what they knew to be a deliberate lie? If they had themselves taken the body of Jesus, to go on and preach that he had been raised from the dead would be knowingly to spread a planned deception. But the thing is that they didn't only preach it; they suffered for it. They were prepared to go to prison, to be flogged – and even to be put to death. And for what? Something they knew to be a blatant untruth?

This simply does not ring true. It is so unlikely as to be virtually impossible. If anything is clear from the Gospels and the Acts, it is that the apostles were sincere. They may have been deceived, if you like, but they were not deceivers. Hypocrites and martyrs are not made of the same stuff.

The fifth and perhaps the least unreasonable (though still hypothetical) explanation of the disappearance of Christ's body is that *the Roman or Jewish authorities took it into their own custody.* They would certainly have had sufficient motive for doing so. They had heard that Jesus had talked about being raised from the dead, and were afraid that someone would pretend it had happened. So (the argument runs), in order to forestall trickery, they took the precaution of confiscating the corpse.

But when it is examined, this hypothetical reconstruction of what happened also falls apart. We have already seen that, not long after Jesus' death, the Christians were boldly proclaiming his resurrection. The news spread rapidly. This new movement threatened to undermine the foundations of Judaism and to disturb the peace of Jerusalem. The Jews feared conversions; the Romans were apprehensive about riots. The authorities had one obvious course of action available to them. They could produce the remains of the body and publish a statement of what they had done.

*What the authorities **didn't** say is as clear a pointer to the truth of the resurrection as what the apostles **did** say.*

Instead, they were silent and resorted to violence. They arrested the apostles, threatened them, flogged them, imprisoned them, belittled them, plotted against them, and even killed some of them. But all this was entirely unnecessary if they had in their own possession the dead body of Jesus. The church was founded on the resurrection. Disprove the resurrection, and the church would have collapsed. But they couldn't, because they didn't have the body. What the authorities *didn't* say is as clear a pointer to the truth of the resurrection as what the apostles *did* say.

These are the theories which have been invented to try to explain the emptiness of the tomb and the disappearance of the body. None of them is satisfactory. None of them can be backed up by any historical evidence. Since there is no adequate alternative explanation, is it not entirely reasonable to prefer the uncomplicated and restrained account we find in the Gospels, setting out the events of the first Easter Day? The body of Jesus was not removed by people; it was raised by God.

THE GRAVECLOTHES WERE UNDISTURBED

It is a remarkable fact that the accounts which say that the body of Jesus had gone also tell us that the strips of linen used to wrap the body had not gone. It is John who lays particular emphasis on this fact, for he went with Peter on that dramatic early morning race to the tomb. The account he gives of this incident (20:1–10) bears the unmistakable marks of first-hand experience. He got there before Peter, but on arriving at the tomb he did no more than look in, until Peter came and entered it. 'Finally the other disciple, who had reached the tomb first, also went inside. He saw and believed.' The question is: what did he see which made him believe? The story suggests that it was not just the absence of the body, but the presence of the strips of linen and, in particular, the fact that they were undisturbed.

Let us try to reconstruct the story.[2] John tells us (19:38–42) that, while Joseph asked Pilate for the body of Jesus, Nicodemus 'brought a mixture of myrrh and aloes, about seventy-five pounds. Taking Jesus' body, the two of them wrapped it, with the spices, in strips of linen. This was in accordance with Jewish burial customs.' That is to say, as they wound the linen 'bandages' round his body, they sprinkled the powdered spices into the folds. A separate cloth will have been used for his head.[3] In this way they wrapped his body and head completely, leaving just his face and neck bare, according to oriental custom. They then laid the body on a stone slab which had been hewn out of the side of the cave-tomb.

Now supposing we had been present in the tomb when the resurrection of Jesus actually took place. What would we have seen? Should we have seen Jesus begin to move, and then yawn and stretch and get up? No. We do not believe that he returned to this life. He did not recover consciousness after a faint. He had died, and he rose again. His was a resurrection, not a resuscitation. We believe that he passed miraculously from death into an altogether new sphere of existence. What then should we have seen, had we been there? We should suddenly have noticed that the body had disappeared. It would have been transformed into something new and different and wonderful. It would have passed through the graveclothes, as it was later to pass through closed doors, leaving them untouched and almost undisturbed. Almost, but not quite. For the strips of linen, under the weight of all those spices, once the support of the body had been removed, would have subsided or collapsed, and would now be lying flat. A gap would have appeared between the strips of linen used for the body and the cloth wrapped around the head, where his face and neck had been. And the head cloth itself, because of the complicated criss-cross pattern of the bandages, might well have retained its concave shape, a crumpled turban, but with no head inside it.

A careful study of the text of John's narrative suggests that it is just these three characteristics of the discarded graveclothes which he saw. First, he saw the strips of linen 'lying there'. The word is repeated twice, and the first time it is placed in an emphatic position in the Greek sentence. We might translate, 'He saw, as they were lying (or 'collapsed'), the strips of linen.' Next, the head cloth was 'still lying in its place, separate from the linen' (TNIV). This is unlikely to mean that it had been bundled up and tossed into a corner. It lay still on the stone slab, but was separated from the body cloths by a noticeable space. Third, this same head cloth was 'lying in its place . . .' This last word has been translated 'twirled', a word which aptly describes the rounded shape which the empty head cloth still preserved.

It is not hard to imagine the sight which greeted the eyes of the apostles when they reached the tomb: the stone slab, the collapsed graveclothes, the shell of the head cloth and the gap between the two. No wonder they 'saw and believed'. A glance at these graveclothes both proved the reality of what had happened and indicated the nature of the resurrection. The strips of linen hadn't been touched, folded or manipulated by any human being. They were like a discarded chrysalis from which the butterfly has emerged.

That the state of the graveclothes was intended to be visible, corroborative evidence for the resurrection is further suggested by the fact that Mary Magdalene (who had returned to the tomb after bringing the news to Peter and John) 'bent over to look into the tomb and saw two angels in white, seated where Jesus' body had been, one at the head and the other at the foot'. Presumably this means that they sat on the stone slab with the graveclothes between them. Both Matthew and Mark add that one of them said, 'He is not here; he has risen, just as he said. Come and see the place where he lay.'[4] Whether or not we believe in angels, these allusions to the place where Jesus had been laid down, emphasized both by where the angels were and by what the angels said, at least confirm what the Gospel writers thought. The position of the strips of linen and the absence of the body were both witnesses together to his resurrection.

JESUS WAS SEEN

The Gospels include some extraordinary stories of how Jesus appeared to his disciples after his resurrection. We are told of ten separate appearances of the risen Lord to what Peter calls 'chosen witnesses'. It is said that he appeared to Mary Magdalene, to the women returning from the tomb, to Peter, to two disciples on the road to Emmaus, to the ten gathered in the upper room, to the eleven including Thomas a week later, to 'more than five hundred brothers and sisters at one time', probably on the mountainside in Galilee, to James, to some disciples including Peter, Thomas, Nathanael, James and John by the side of Lake Galilee, and to many on the Mount of Olives near Bethany at the time of the ascension. Paul adds himself at the end of his list of those who saw the risen Jesus in 1 Corinthians 15, referring to his experience on the Damascus Road. And since Luke tells us at the beginning of the Acts that Jesus 'presented himself to them and gave many convincing proofs that he was alive' and 'appeared to them [the apostles] over a period of forty days', there may well have been other appearances, of which no record has survived.

We cannot lightly dismiss this body of living evidence about the resurrection. We must find some explanation of what these accounts are telling us. Only three are possible. One is that they were inventions; the second that they were hallucinations; the third that they were true.

Were they *inventions*? There is no need to devote much space to repudiating this suggestion. The resurrection appearances cannot be deliberate inventions. For one thing, the narratives are restrained and simple; for another, they are graphic and brought to life by the detailed touches which sound like the work of an eyewitness. The stories of the race to the tomb in John 20 and of the walk to Emmaus in Luke 24 are too vivid and real to have been invented.

Besides, if they *are* inventions, they're certainly not very good ones. If we had wanted to concoct the resurrection, we could probably have done much better ourselves! We should have been careful to avoid the complicated jigsaw puzzle of events which the four Gospels together produce. We should have got rid of, or at least watered down, the doubts and fears of the apostles. We should probably have included a dramatic account of the resurrection itself, describing the power and glory of the Son of God as he snapped the chains of death and burst out of the tomb in triumph. But no-one saw it happen, and we have no description of it. Again, we would have chosen someone with a better reputation than Mary Magdalene as the first witness.

Actually, there is an even weightier objection to the theory of invention than the naïve simplicity of the narratives. It is the obvious fact, which we have already mentioned, that the apostles, together with the Gospel writers in particular and the early church in general, were utterly convinced that Jesus had risen. The whole New Testament breathes an atmosphere of certainty and conquest. Its writers may have been, if you like, tragically misled; they were definitely not deliberately misleading.

If these accounts were not inventions, were the appearances themselves *hallucinations*? This opinion has been widely held and confidently expressed; and of course hallucinations are not an uncommon phenomenon. A hallucination is the 'apparent perception of an external object when no such object is present', and is associated most frequently with someone who is suffering from some form of mental ill health. Most of us have known people who see things and hear voices, and live sometimes or always in an imaginary world of their own. It is simply not credible to claim that the apostles were unbalanced people like this. Mary Magdalene may have been, but hardly blustering Peter and doubting Thomas.

It is true that hallucinations can occur in people who are otherwise quite ordinary and normal, but such cases are usually associated with two particular characteristics. First, they happen as the climax to a period of exaggerated wishful thinking. Second, the conditions of time, place and mood are favourable. There must be both a strong inward desire and a set of predisposing outward circumstances.

When we look at the Gospel narratives of the resurrection, however, both these factors are missing. Far from wishful thinking, it was just the opposite. When the women first found the tomb empty, they were 'trembling and bewildered', they fled from the scene and they were 'afraid'. When Mary Magdalene and the other women reported that Jesus was alive, we read that the apostles 'did not believe the women, because their words seemed to them like nonsense'. When Jesus himself came and stood among them 'they were startled and frightened, thinking they saw a ghost', so that Jesus 'rebuked them for their lack of faith and their stubborn refusal to believe'. Thomas was adamant in his refusal to believe unless he could actually see and touch the nail-wounds. When Jesus later met the eleven and others on a mountain in Galilee, 'they worshipped him; but some doubted'. There was no wishful thinking here, no naïve credulity, no blind acceptance. Far from being gullible and easily led, the disciples were cautious, sceptical and 'slow to believe'. They were not susceptible to hallucinations. Nor would strange visions have satisfied them. Their faith was grounded upon the hard facts of experience that could be verified.

Not only this, but the outwardly favourable circumstances were missing too. Had the appearances all taken place in one or two particularly sacred places, hallowed by memories of Jesus, and had those who saw him been expecting to do so, our suspicions might well be aroused. If we had only the story of the appearances in the upper room, we should have good reason to doubt and ask questions. It's not hard to imagine the eleven disciples gathering in the special place where Jesus had spent some of his last hours with them. We can picture them keeping his place vacant, talking together over old times and remembering his promises to return. It's not too much of a leap to think of them beginning to wonder if he might come back after all, and then hoping that he would, until the eagerness of their expectation was rewarded by his sudden appearance. It would be a cruel delusion, yes, but an understandable one.

But this was not the case. Indeed, an investigation of the ten appearances reveals a striking variety in the circumstances of person, place and mood in which they occurred. He was seen by individuals alone (Mary Magdalene, Peter and James), by small groups and by more than five hundred people together. He appeared in the garden of the tomb, near Jerusalem, in the upper room, on the road to Emmaus, by the lake of Galilee, on a Galilee mountain and on the Mount of Olives.

If there was variety in person and place, there was also variety in mood. Mary Magdalene was weeping; the other women were afraid and astonished; Peter was full of remorse, and Thomas of scepticism. The Emmaus pair were distracted by the events of the week and the disciples in Galilee by their fishing. Yet through their doubts and fears, through their unbelief and preoccupation, the risen Lord made himself known to them.

It is unreasonable to dismiss these appearances of Jesus as hallucinations being experienced by people with disturbed minds. So, if they were neither inventions nor hallucinations, the only alternative left is that they actually happened. The risen Lord was seen.

THE DISCIPLES WERE CHANGED

Perhaps the transformation of the disciples of Jesus is the greatest evidence of all for the resurrection, because it is entirely uncontrived. They do not invite us to look at themselves, as they invite us to look at the empty tomb and the collapsed graveclothes and the Lord whom they had seen. We can see the change in them without being asked to look. The men who figure in the pages of the Gospels are new and different men in the Acts of the Apostles, the New Testament book which tells the story of the first Christians. The death of their Master left them despondent, disillusioned, and near to despair. But in the Acts they emerge as those who risk their lives for the name of the Lord Jesus Christ and who turn the world upside down.

What has brought about such a change? How can we account for their new faith and power, joy and love? There's no doubt that the events of Pentecost and the coming of the Holy Spirit had a lot to do with it. But the Holy Spirit came only when Jesus had risen and returned to heaven. It is as if the resurrection was the key which unlocked extraordinary moral and spiritual power. Two examples stand out.

The first is Simon Peter. The story of the trial and death of Jesus has been a complete nightmare for him. He has denied Christ three times. He has cursed and sworn as if he had never known the gentle influence of Jesus in his life. He has gone out into the night to weep bitterly. When Jesus is dead, he joins the others in the upper room, behind barred doors 'for fear of the Jews', and is utterly dejected.

But when we turn over one or two pages in the Bible, we see him standing, perhaps on the steps outside the very same house in Jerusalem, preaching so boldly and so powerfully to a vast crowd that three thousand people believe in Christ and are baptized. We turn on to the next chapters of the Acts and we watch him defying the very Sanhedrin who had condemned Jesus to death just a few weeks earlier, happy to be counted worthy to suffer shame for his name, and later calmly sleeping in his cell on the night before his expected execution.

He is a new man. The shifting sands have been blown away; true to the meaning of his nickname, 'Peter', he is a real rock now. What has made the difference?

Or take James, who later occupied a position of leadership in the Jerusalem church. He is one of 'the brothers of the Lord', who are represented throughout the Gospels as not believing in Jesus: 'Even his brothers did not believe in him.' But when we reach the first chapter of the Acts, the list which Luke gives of the disciples gathered together ends with the words 'and . . . his brothers'. James is evidently a believer now. What has made the difference? What convinced him? Perhaps we have the clue we are seeking in 1 Corinthians 15:7 where Paul, cataloguing those who had seen the risen Jesus, adds 'he appeared to James'.

It was the resurrection which transformed Peter's fear into courage, and James's doubt into faith. It was the resurrection which changed the Jewish Sabbath into the Christian Sunday. It was the resurrection which changed Saul the Pharisee into Paul the apostle, the fanatical persecutor into a preacher of the very faith he previously tried to destroy. 'Last of all', Paul wrote, 'he appeared to me also.'

These are the strands of the evidence for the resurrection. The body had disappeared. The graveclothes remained undisturbed. The Lord was seen. And the disciples were changed. There is no adequate explanation of these events other than the great Christian affirmation: 'The Lord is risen indeed.'

Over these last three chapters we have undertaken a careful investigation of the most absorbing personality of history, a modest carpenter from Nazareth who became a peasant preacher and died a criminal's death.

- His claims were astonishing.
- He seems to have been morally perfect.
- He rose from the dead.

Added together, the weight of all this evidence is pretty impressive. It paves the way for the last step of faith where we come to bow before Jesus and say, along with doubting Thomas, 'My Lord and my God.'

STUDY QUESTIONS

1. Why is the claim that Jesus was raised from the dead so important? What does it prove?
2. What are the four statements which summarize the evidence for the resurrection?
3. What explanations have been put forward to account for the empty tomb? What do you make of them?
4. What is so remarkable about the fact that the graveclothes were undisturbed?

5. How would you answer someone who said that the appearances of Jesus after his resurrection were inventions or hallucinations?

6. What does the experience of the disciples of Jesus contribute to our ability to believe that he was raised from the dead?

PART TWO:

WHAT WE NEED

Chapter 5

THE FACT AND NATURE OF SIN

We have looked in some detail at the evidence for the unique deity of Jesus of Nazareth. As a result, we may well have become convinced that, yes, he is indeed the Lord, the Son of God. Yet the focus of the New Testament is not just on who he was, but on what he came to do. He is presented not simply as the Lord from heaven, but also as the Saviour of sinners. Indeed, the two cannot be separated, for the effectiveness of what he did depends absolutely on the truth of who he was.

But in order to appreciate what exactly it was that Jesus achieved, we need to understand who *we* are as well as who *he* was. His work was done for us. It was the work of a person for persons, a mission undertaken for needy people by the only one who was able to meet their need. His ability lies in his deity; our need lies in our sin. We have investigated his claim to be able to help us; we must now look at the nature of the help we need.

So we turn from Christ in particular to humanity in general, from what the Bible reveals about the sinlessness and glory that are in him to what it has to say about the sin and shame that are in us. Only then, after we have clearly grasped what we are, shall we be in a position to perceive the wonder of what he has done for us and offers to us. We need to be convinced about the accuracy of the diagnosis before we will be ready to take the medicine God prescribes.

Sin is an unpopular subject, and Christians are often criticized for going on about it too much. But they only do so because they are realists. Sin is not a convenient invention of church ministers to keep them in their job; it is a fact of human experience.

The history of the last hundred years or so has convinced many people that the problem of evil is located in human beings themselves, not merely in human society. The nineteenth century saw a flourishing of liberal optimism. It was widely believed that human nature was fundamentally good, that evil was largely caused by ignorance and bad housing, and that education and social reform would enable people to live together in happiness and goodwill. But this illusion has been shattered by the hard facts of history. Educational opportunities have spread rapidly throughout the world, and many welfare states have been created. But our human capacity to get it wrong seems undaunted. The persistence of conflict on the world stage and the widespread denial of human rights, together with the general increase of violence and crime, have forced thoughtful people to acknowledge that a hard core of selfishness exists in each and every one of us.

Much that we take for granted in a 'civilized' society is actually based upon the assumption of human sin. Nearly all legislation has grown up because we simply cannot be trusted to settle our disputes with justice and without self-interest. A promise is not enough; we need a contract. Doors are not enough; we have to lock and bolt them. The payment of fares is not enough; tickets have to be issued, inspected and collected. Law and order are not enough; we need the police to enforce them. All this is due to our sin. We cannot trust one another. We need protection against one another. It is a terrible indication of what human nature is really like.

THE UNIVERSALITY OF SIN

The Bible writers are quite clear that sin is universal. 'There is no-one who does not sin,' says King Solomon in an aside during his great prayer at the dedication of the temple in Jerusalem. 'Indeed, there is no-one on earth who is righteous, no-one who does what is right and never sins,' adds the Preacher in the book of Ecclesiastes (TNIV). Several of the psalms comment sadly on the universality of human sin. Psalm 14, which describes the godless 'fool', gives a very pessimistic description of human wickedness:

> They are corrupt, their deeds are vile;
>   there is no-one who does good.
> The LORD looks down from heaven
>   on the human race
> to see if there are any who understand,
>   any who seek God.
> All have turned away,
>   all have become corrupt;
> there is no-one who does good,
>   not even one.

The psalmists' conscience tells them that if God were to rise up in judgment against humanity, none could escape his condemnation. 'If you, LORD, kept a record of sins, Lord, who could stand?' (TNIV) Hence the prayer, 'Do not bring your servant into judgment, for no-one living is righteous before you.'

The prophets are as insistent as the psalmists on the fact that all people are sinners, and no statements are more definite than the two which are to be found in the second half of the book of Isaiah. 'We all, like sheep, have gone astray, each of us has turned to our own way' (TNIV), and 'All of us have become like one who is unclean, and all our righteous acts are like filthy rags.'

It isn't only the Old Testament writers who share this view. Paul opens his letter to the Romans with a closely reasoned argument, which extends over the first three chapters, that everyone, no matter who they are, is a sinner in God's sight. He writes about the corrupt behaviour of the pagan world and then adds that his own people, the people of Israel, are no better. They have been entrusted with God's holy law – and even teach it to others. Yet they break it just as much as anyone else. Paul goes on to quote from the psalms and the prophet Isaiah to illustrate his theme, and concludes, 'There is no difference [between Jew and Gentile], for all have sinned and fall short of the glory of God.' John, another New Testament writer, is, if anything, even more explicit when he declares, 'If we claim to be without sin, we deceive ourselves,' and 'If we claim we have not sinned, we make him out to be a liar.'[1]

But what is sin? Yes, it affects everyone – but what exactly is it? Several words are used in the Bible to describe its nature. They can be put into two groups, according to whether wrongdoing is seen negatively or positively. Negatively, it is shortcoming. One word represents it as a lapse, a slip, a blunder. Another pictures it as the failure to hit a target. Yet another shows it to be an inner badness, having a character which falls short of what is good.

Positively, sin is wrongdoing. One word describes sin as trespassing over a boundary. Another reveals it as failing to keep the law, and another as an act which contravenes justice.

Both these groups of words imply the existence of a clear standard of behaviour. It is either an ideal which we fail to reach, or a law which we break. 'Anyone ... who knows the good he ought to do and doesn't do it, sins,' says James. That is the negative aspect. 'Everyone who sins breaks the law; in fact, sin is lawlessness,' says John. That is the positive aspect.

The Bible accepts the fact that people have different standards. The people of Israel have the law of Moses. Everyone else has the law of conscience. But everyone has broken the law they know. Everyone has fallen short of their own standard. What is our ethical code? It may be the law of Moses or the teaching of Jesus. It may be the decent thing, or the done thing, or the conventions of society. It may be Buddhism's eightfold path or Islam's five pillars of conduct. But whatever it is, we have not succeeded in observing it. We all stand self-condemned.

This comes as a genuine surprise to many people. They have their ideals and think they achieve them, more or less. They do not go in for introspection. They are not unduly self-critical. They know they have had occasional lapses. They are aware of certain character defects. But they are not particularly worried by them, and think of themselves as no worse than anyone else. All this is understandable enough, until we remember two things. First, our sense of success or failure depends on how high our standards are. We'd find it quite easy to consider ourselves good at high-jumping if the bar were never raised more than a few inches! Secondly, God is interested in the thought behind the deed and the motive behind the action.

Jesus clearly taught this in the Sermon on the Mount, set out for us in chapters 5 to 7 of Matthew's Gospel. With these two principles in mind, a healthy exercise would be to take the Ten Commandments in Exodus 20 as our standard and see how very far short of it we all fall.

THE TEN COMMANDMENTS

1. You shall have no other gods before me

This is God's demand for our exclusive worship. We don't have to worship the sun, the moon and the stars to break this law. We break it whenever we give to something or someone other than God himself the first place in our thoughts or our affections. It may be some engrossing sport, an absorbing hobby, or selfish ambition. Or it may be someone whom we idolize. We may worship a god of gold and silver in the form of safe investments and a healthy bank balance, or a god of wood and stone in the form of property and possessions. None of these things is necessarily wrong in itself. It becomes wrong only when we give to it the place in our lives which belongs only to God. Sin is basically the placing of self where God should be. The way a wit once described the typical Victorian Englishman is true of us all: 'a self-made man who worships his creator'.

For us to keep this first commandment would be, as Jesus said, to love the Lord our God with all our heart and with all our soul and with all our mind; to make his will our guide and his glory our goal; to put him first in thought, word and deed; in work and leisure; in friendships and career; in the use of our money, time and talents; at work and at home. No-one has ever kept this commandment except Jesus of Nazareth.

2. *You shall not make for yourself an image*

If the first commandment is about *what* we worship, the second is about *how* we worship. In the first God demands our exclusive worship, and in the second our sincere and spiritual worship. For 'God is spirit, and his worshippers must worship in the Spirit and in truth.'[2]

We may never have manufactured some statue or figurine and bowed down to worship it, but what distorted mental images of God do we hold in our minds? And although this commandment does not forbid the use of all external forms in worship, it does imply that they are useless unless there is inward reality as well. We may have attended church – but have we ever really worshipped God? We may have said prayers – but have we ever really prayed? We may have read the Bible – but have we ever let God speak to us through it and have we done what he said? It is no good approaching God with our lips if our hearts are far from him.[3] To do so is sheer hypocrisy.

3. *You shall not misuse the name of the Lord your God*

The name of God represents the nature of God. This is why there is so much in the Bible which tells us to respect his name, and why in the Lord's Prayer we are taught to pray that his name may be 'hallowed' or kept special. His holy name can be dragged in the mud by our careless use of language, and most of us would do well to revise our vocabulary from time to time. But to take God's name in vain is not just a matter of words – it's also about thoughts and deeds. Whenever our behaviour is inconsistent with our belief, when what we do contradicts what we say, we take God's name in vain. To call God 'Lord' and disobey him is to take his name in vain. To call God 'Father' and be filled with anxiety and doubts is to deny his name. To take God's name in vain is to talk one way and act another. This too is hypocrisy.

4. Remember the Sabbath day by keeping it holy

The Jews' Sabbath and the Christians' Sunday are part of what God has put in place for us. To set apart one day in seven is not just a human arrangement or a social convenience. It is God's plan. He made the Sabbath for people, Jesus emphasized,[4] and since he also made the people for whom he made the Sabbath, he adapted it to people's needs. Our bodies and minds need rest, and our spirits need the opportunity for worship. This is why the Sabbath is set aside as a day of rest and a day of worship.

Not only are we to keep it like this ourselves, for our own good, but we are to do all we can for the common good to ensure that others do not have to work unnecessarily on this day.

So Sunday is a 'holy' day, set apart for God. It is the Lord's day, not our day. It should therefore be spent in his way, not in ours, to worship and serve him – and not just for our self-centred pleasure.

5. Honour your father and your mother

This fifth commandment still comes in the first half of the law which is all about our duty to God. For our parents, at least while we are children, represent God's authority to us. Yet often it is in their own homes that people, young people especially, can be at their most selfish and inconsiderate. It is all too easy to be ungrateful and negligent, and to fail to show our parents due respect and affection. How often do we contact them or visit them? Or do they need support of one kind or another which we could give, but fail to make available to them?

6. You shall not murder

This is not just about the crime of murder. After all, if looks could kill, many would kill with a look. And if murder can be committed by cutting words, many are clearly guilty. Indeed Jesus said that to be angry with someone without good reason, or to be insulting, are as serious as actually killing someone. John draws the right conclusion when he writes, 'Anyone who hates a fellow believer is a murderer' (1 John 3:15 TNIV). Every loss of temper, every outburst of uncontrolled passion, every stirring of sullen rage, every bitter resentment and thirsting for revenge – all these things are murder. We can kill by malicious gossip. We can kill by studied neglect and cruelty. We can kill by spite and jealousy. We have probably all done so.

7. You shall not commit adultery

Again, this commandment has a far wider application than being unfaithful in marriage. It includes any sort of sex outside the marriage relationship for which it was designed. It also includes all sexual perversions, for although men and women are not necessarily responsible for the urges they have, they are responsible for what they do about them. It includes selfish demands within marriage, and any behaviour which drives a partner to want to end the relationship. It includes the use of pornography, and giving in to impure fantasies. Jesus made this clear when he said, 'Anyone who looks at a woman lustfully has already committed adultery with her in his heart.'

Just as to think murderous thoughts is to commit murder, so to think adulterous thoughts is to commit adultery. This commandment embraces every abuse of a sacred and beautiful gift of God.

8. You shall not steal

To steal is to rob a person of anything which belongs to him or is due to him. Taking money or property is not the only way in which this commandment can be broken. Tax evasion is robbery. So is dodging the customs. So is working short hours. What people call 'scrounging', God calls stealing. To overwork and underpay your staff is to break this commandment. There can be few of us, if any, who have been thoroughly honest in personal and business affairs.

These negative commandments also imply a positive counterpart. In order truly to avoid murder, we must do all we can to promote the health and support the life of others. It isn't enough to refrain from the act of adultery. The commandment requires the right, healthy and honourable attitude of each sex towards the other. Similarly, not stealing is no particular virtue if we are miserly or mean. In his New Testament letter to the Ephesians, Paul makes the point that it isn't enough for thieves to stop stealing; they must also start working. And he says this not just so that they can provide for their own needs, but also so that they may have something to share with those in need.

9. You shall not give false testimony against your neighbour

The last five commandments express a respect for the rights of others which is implied in true love. To break these commandments is to rob people of the things most precious to them – life ('you shall not murder'), their home or honour ('you shall not commit adultery'), their property ('you shall not steal'), and now their reputation ('you shall not give false testimony against your neighbour').

This commandment doesn't only apply in a court of law. It does include perjury. But it also refers to all forms of scandal, slander, idle talk and gossip, all lies and deliberate exaggerations or distortions of the truth. We can give false testimony by listening to unkind rumours as well as by passing them on, by making cruel jokes at somebody else's expense, by creating false impressions, by failing to correct statements which we know to be untrue, and by what we do *not* say as well as by what we *do* say.

10. You shall not covet

The tenth commandment is in some ways the most revealing of all. It turns the Ten Commandments from an external legal code into an internal moral standard. We can be brought to book by the law of the land for theft – but not for covetousness. For covetousness belongs to the inner life. It lurks in the heart and the mind. What lust is to adultery and temper is to murder, covetousness is to theft.

So much takes place beneath the surface of our lives . . . But God sees these things. His eye penetrates into every corner of our hearts.

The particular things which we are not to covet and which are mentioned in the commandment are surprisingly modern. In the housing shortage there is much coveting of our neighbour's house, and divorce would not be so common if people did not covet their neighbour's wife or husband. 'Greed . . . is idolatry,' wrote Paul, and by contrast, 'godliness with contentment is great gain'.

Listing these commandments brings to light an ugly catalogue of sins. So much takes place beneath the surface of our lives, in the secret places of our minds, which other people do not see and which we manage to conceal even from ourselves. But God sees these things. His eye penetrates into every corner of our hearts: 'Nothing in all creation is hidden from God's sight. Everything is uncovered and laid bare before the eyes of him to whom we must give account.' He sees us as we really are, and his law shows up our sins for what they really are. Indeed, the purpose of the law was to expose sin, for 'through the law we become conscious of sin'.

When C. H. Spurgeon, a famous nineteenth-century preacher, was only fourteen years old, he experienced a tremendous sense of his own sinfulness. Two truths came home to him as never before: 'God's majesty and my sinfulness'. He had a crushing sense of how unworthy he was.

> I do not hesitate to say that those who examined my life would not have seen any extraordinary sin, yet as I looked upon *myself* I saw outrageous sin against God. I was not like other boys, untruthful, dishonest, swearing and so on. But of a sudden, I met Moses carrying the law ... God's Ten Words ... and as I read them, they all seemed to join in condemning me in the sight of the thrice holy Jehovah.

In our case, too, there is nothing like the law of God for convincing us of our sinfulness.

STUDY QUESTIONS

1. Why is sin such an unpopular subject?
2. Why does an investigation into basic Christianity need to examine sin so carefully?
3. How does the Bible underline the universality of sin?
4. If you had to define what sin is, what would you say?
5. In what ways are the Ten Commandments useful for us today?

Chapter 6

THE CONSEQUENCES OF SIN

We have looked at the universality and the nature of human sin. We might prefer to leave this unpleasant subject and pass on immediately to the good news of Christ's salvation, but we are not yet ready to do so. We need to grasp what the results of sin are before we can fully appreciate what God has done for us and what he offers to us in Christ.

Is sin really so very serious? The best way to understand its evil consequences is to look at its effects on God, on ourselves and on other people.

ALIENATION FROM GOD
Even though we may not realize it now, the most terrible result of sin is that it cuts us off from God. Our highest destiny is to know God, to be in personal relationship with him. Our chief claim to nobility as human beings is that we were made in the image of God and are therefore capable of knowing him. But

this God whom we are meant to know and whom we ought to know is a righteous Being, infinite in his moral perfection. The Bible consistently stresses this truth:

> For this is what the high and exalted One says –
> he who lives forever, whose name is holy:
> 'I live in a high and holy place...'

> The King of kings and Lord of lords, who ... lives in unapproachable light.

> God is light; in him there is no darkness at all. If we claim to have fellowship with him yet walk in the darkness, we lie and do not live by the truth.

> Our God is a consuming fire.

> Who of us can dwell with the consuming fire?
> Who of us can dwell with everlasting burning?

> Your eyes are too pure to look on evil;
> you cannot tolerate wrong.[1]

All the individuals in the Bible who have caught a glimpse of God's glory have drawn back from the sight, overwhelmed by the awareness of their own sins. *Moses*, to whom God appeared in the bush that was on fire but was not burnt up, 'hid his face, because he was afraid to look at God'. *Job*, to whom God spoke 'out of the storm' in words which revealed the full extent of his majesty, cried out, 'My ears had heard of you but now my eyes have seen you. Therefore I despise myself and repent in dust and ashes.' *Isaiah*, a young man at the threshold of his career, had a vision of God as the King of Israel 'seated on a throne, high and exalted', surrounded by worshipping angels who sang of his holiness and glory, and said, 'Woe to me! I am ruined! For I am a man of unclean lips, and I live among a people of unclean lips, and my eyes have seen the King, the LORD Almighty.' When *Ezekiel* received his strange vision of living winged creatures and whirring wheels, and above them a throne, and on the throne a figure like that of a man, enveloped in the brightness of fire and of the rainbow, he recognized it as 'the appearance of the likeness of the glory of the LORD', and he added, 'When I saw it, I fell face down.' *Saul of Tarsus*, travelling to Damascus, mad with rage against the Christians, was struck to the ground and blinded by a brilliant light which flashed from heaven more brightly than the sun, and wrote later of his vision of the risen Christ, 'He appeared to me also.' The aged *John*, exiled on the island of Patmos, describes in detail his vision of the risen Jesus in heaven, whose 'eyes were like blazing fire' and whose 'face was like the sun shining in all its brilliance', and he tells us, 'When I saw him, I fell at his feet as though dead.'[2]

If the curtain which veils the indescribable majesty of God could be drawn aside – even for a moment – we too would be unable to bear the sight. As it is, we're only dimly aware of how pure and brilliant the glory of almighty God must be. However, we know enough to realize that we could never approach such a God while still in our sins. A great chasm yawns between God in his holiness and us in our sin. 'For what do righteousness and wickedness have in common? Or what fellowship can light have with darkness?' asks Paul.

The fact that sin cuts us off from God was brought home dramatically in Old Testament times by the way the tabernacle and the temple were constructed. Both these structures, designed to house the presence of God among his people, were made in two compartments. The first and larger one was called the Holy Place, while the further and smaller area was known as the Most Holy Place or the Holy of Holies. In this inner sanctuary was what was called the Shekinah glory, the visible symbol of God's presence. Between the two was the 'veil', a thick curtain which barred access into the Holy of Holies. No-one was allowed to pass through into God's presence except the high priest, and he only on the annual Day of Atonement and then only if he took with him the blood of a sacrifice for sins.

What was visibly demonstrated to the Israelites in this way is underlined by the teaching we find in the Old and the New Testaments. Sin brings inevitable separation, and this separation is 'death', spiritual death, the cutting off of a person from God, the only source of true life. 'The wages of sin is death.'

More than that, if in this life we deliberately reject Jesus Christ, the only one through whom we may find eternal life, we will die eternally in the next world. Hell is a grim and dreadful reality. We must not let ourselves be deceived about this. Jesus himself spoke of it. He called it 'darkness' because it is an infinite separation from God who is light. The Bible also calls it 'the second death' and 'the lake of fire', terms which describe symbolically the loss of eternal life and the dreadful thirst of the soul which are the inevitable result of being banished from God's presence.[3]

This separation from God which is caused by sin is not only taught in the Bible; it is confirmed by human experience. I can still remember my own sense of confusion when as a boy I said my prayers and tried to enter God's presence. I could not understand why God seemed so far away and I could not get near him. He seemed so remote and distant. I know the reason now. Isaiah has given me the answer:

Surely the arm of the LORD is not too short to save,
    nor his ear too dull to hear.
But your iniquities have separated
    you from your God;
your sins have hidden his face from you,
    so that he will not hear.[4]

We are tempted to say to God, as does the writer of the book of
Lamentations, 'You have covered yourself with a cloud so that
no prayer can get through.' But in fact God is not responsible
for the cloud. We are. Our sins blot out God's face from us as
effectively as the clouds cover
the sun.

Many people have told me
that they have had the same
bleak experience. Sometimes,
in emergencies, in danger, in
joy or in the contemplation of
beauty, they feel that God is
near to them. But, more often
than not, they find God to be
inexplicably absent, and they
feel abandoned. This is not just

*Our sins blot
out God's face
from us as effectively
as the clouds cover
the sun.*

a feeling; it is a fact. Until our sins are forgiven, we are indeed
exiles, far from our true home. We have no relationship with
God. In biblical terms we are 'lost', or 'dead through the
transgressions and sins' which we have committed.

It is this that accounts for the restlessness of men and women
today. There is a hunger in our hearts which only God can
satisfy, a vacuum which only he can fill. The demand for
sensational news, extravagant love or crime stories in the
media; the current epidemic of drugs, sex and violence – all

these things are symptoms of our search for satisfaction. They betray our thirst for God and our separation from him. Augustine was right in the often-quoted words which come near the beginning of his *Confessions*: 'You have made us for yourself, and our hearts are restless till they find their rest in you.' This situation is tragic beyond words. We are missing the destiny for which God made us.

BONDAGE TO SELF

Sin not only alienates; it enslaves. It separates us from God and it also brings us into captivity.

We need now to consider the 'inwardness' of sin. It is more than the wrong things we do; it is a deep-seated inner sickness. In fact, the sins we commit are merely the external and visible indications of this internal and invisible illness, the symptoms of a moral disease. The image Jesus used is that of a tree and its fruit. The kind of fruit a tree bears, he said (whether figs or grapes, for example), and their condition (whether good or bad), depend on the nature and health of the tree itself. 'For out of the overflow of the heart the mouth speaks.'

In this respect, Jesus Christ is at odds with many modern commentators. It is certainly true that we are all influenced for good or ill by our education and environment, and by the political and economic system under which we live. It is also true that we should seek justice, freedom and well-being for our fellow human beings. Yet Jesus did not attribute the evils of human society to these. According to him, the problem lies with our very nature, with what he called our 'heart'. Here are his exact words:

> For from within, out of your hearts, come evil thoughts, sexual immorality, theft, murder, adultery, greed, malice, deceit, lewdness,

envy, slander, arrogance and folly. All these evils come from inside and defile you.[5]

The Old Testament had already taught this truth. As Jeremiah put it, 'The heart is deceitful above all things and beyond cure. Who can understand it?' Indeed, the Bible contains many references to this infection of human nature – what we call 'original sin'. It is a tendency or bias of self-centredness, which we inherit, which is rooted deeply in our human personality, and which reveals itself in a thousand ugly ways. Paul's label for it is 'the sinful nature', and he sets out a catalogue of what it produces.

The acts of the sinful nature are obvious: sexual immorality, impurity and debauchery; idolatry and witchcraft; hatred, discord, jealousy, fits of rage, selfish ambition, dissensions, factions and envy; drunkenness, orgies, and the like.[6]

It is because sin is an internal sickness of human nature that we are in bondage. It is not so much particular acts or habits which enslave us, but rather the evil infection from which these spring. This is what lies behind the New Testament description of us as 'slaves'. We resent it, but it is true. Jesus really upset some of the religious people of his day when he said to them, 'If you hold to my teaching, you are really my disciples. Then you will know the truth, and the truth will set you free.'

They retorted, 'We are Abraham's descendants and have never been slaves of anyone. How can you say that we shall be set free?'

Jesus answered them, 'I tell you the truth, everyone who sins is a slave to sin.'

In several of his letters Paul describes this humiliation into which sin brings us.

> You used to be slaves to sin.

> All of us also lived among them at one time, gratifying the cravings of our sinful nature and following its desires and thoughts.

> At one time we too were foolish, disobedient, deceived and enslaved by all kinds of passions and pleasures.[7]

The example of our lack of self-discipline which the New Testament writer James focuses on is the difficulty we have in controlling our tongue. In a chapter full of graphic metaphor he says that 'those who are never at fault in what they say are perfect, able to keep their whole body in check'. He points out that 'the tongue is a small part of the body, but it makes great boasts'. Its influence spreads like fire; it is 'a world of evil' and 'corrupts the whole person'. We can tame all kinds of animals and birds, he adds, 'but no-one can tame the tongue'.[8]

We know this only too well. We have high ideals, but weak wills. We want to live a good life, but we are chained in the prison of our self-centredness. However much we may boast of being free, the reality is that we are slaves.

We need to come to God and admit with sorrow:

> It is not finished, Lord,
> There is not one thing done,
> There is no battle of my life
> That I have really won.
> And now I come to tell thee
> How I fought to fail,
> My human, all too human, tale
> Of weakness and futility.[9]

It is no use giving us rules about how to behave; we cannot keep them. However much God might say 'You shall not', we shall – right to the end of time. A lecture will not solve our problem; we need a Saviour. The education of the mind is not enough without a change of heart. Humanity has discovered the secrets of physical power and been able to harness the immense resources of nuclear energy. Now we need spiritual power, to set us free from ourselves, to conquer and control ourselves, the power to give us moral character to match our scientific achievement.

CONFLICT WITH OTHERS

But our list of the terrible consequences of sin is still not complete. There is one more to consider: the effect it has on our relationships with others.

We have seen that sin is a deep-seated infection of human nature. It lies at the root of our personality. It controls our ego. In fact, sin is self. And all the sins we commit are assertions of the self against either God or other people. The Ten Commandments, although a series of negative prohibitions, set out our duty to God and to others. This is made even clearer in the positive summary of God's law which Jesus made when he linked a verse from Leviticus (19:18) to a verse in Deuteronomy (6:5): 'Love the Lord your God with all your heart and with all your soul and with all your mind. This is the first and greatest commandment. And the second is like it: Love your neighbour as yourself. All the Law and the Prophets hang on these two commandments.'

It is important to notice that the first commandment concerns our duty to God, and not our duty to other people. We are to love God first; and then we are to love our neighbour as ourselves. So God's order is that we put him first, others next, self last. Sin is the reversal of the order. It is to put ourselves first, our neighbour next, and God somewhere in the background. Peter Ustinov, who wrote his autobiography and entitled it *Dear Me* was simply giving expression to what we all think of ourselves. When the ice cream is brought into the children's party, the cry goes up, 'Me first!' As we grow up, we learn not to *say* that kind of thing; but we still *think* it. William Temple's way of describing original sin expresses this truth perfectly:

> I am the centre of the world I see; where the horizon is depends on where I stand ... Education may make my self-centredness less disastrous by widening my horizon of interest; so far it is like climbing a tower, which widens the horizon for physical vision, while leaving me still the centre and standard of reference.[10]

This basic self-centredness affects all our behaviour. We do not find it easy to adjust to other people. We tend either to despise them or to envy them, either to feel superior or to consider ourselves inferior. We rarely think of ourselves with the 'sober judgment' which Paul urged upon his readers. Sometimes we are full of inappropriate self-pity, at other times of self-esteem, self-will or self-love.

All the relationships of life are complicated – parents and children, husband and wife, employer and employed. There are many reasons for society's problems with the younger generation, and much is due to lack of security in the home; but the fact is that unruly young people are (for whatever reason) asserting themselves against society. Hundreds of divorces could be prevented if people were humble enough to blame themselves more than their partner. Whenever couples have been to see me because their marriage was under threat,

I have noticed that each tells a different story – a story sometimes so different that one would not guess they were describing the same situation.

Most quarrels are due to a misunderstanding, and the misunderstanding is due to our failure to appreciate the other person's point of view. It is more natural to us to talk than to listen, to argue than to submit. This is true in industrial disputes as much as in domestic quarrels. Many conflicts in the world of employment could be resolved if both sides first examined themselves critically and then examined the other side charitably, rather than our normal practice of being charitable to ourselves and critical of others. The same could be said of complex international unrest. The tensions of today are due largely to fear and foolishness. Our outlook is one-sided. We exaggerate the virtues in ourselves and the vices in others.

It is sadly all too easy to write in this way about social relationships today. The only reason for doing so is to show how human sin or self-centredness is the cause of all our troubles. This is what brings us into conflict with each other. If only the spirit of self-assertion could be replaced by the spirit of self-sacrifice, our conflicts would cease. And self-sacrifice is what the Bible means by 'love'. While sin draws in to itself, love spends itself for others. The characteristic of sin is the desire to get; the characteristic of love is the desire to give.

Love ever gives,
Forgives, outlives,
And ever stands with open hands,
And while it lives it gives.
For this is love's prerogative,
To give – and give – and give.

What man needs is a radical change of nature, what Professor H. M. Gwatkin called 'a change from self to unself'. We cannot do this for ourselves any more than patients needing surgery can perform their own operations. Again, we need a Saviour.

Writing about sin like this has only one purpose. It is to convince us of our need of Jesus Christ, and to help us understand and accept what he offers. Faith is born out of need. We shall never put our trust in Christ until we have first despaired of ourselves. As he himself said, 'It is not the healthy who need a doctor, but the sick. I have not come to call the righteous, but sinners.' Only when we have realized and faced up to the seriousness of what we are suffering from will we admit our urgent need for a cure.

STUDY QUESTIONS

1. How would you respond to the suggestion that sin is not really all that serious?
2. Why does sin have such a catastrophic effect on our relationship with God?
3. Why is slavery such an appropriate image to use when thinking about the effect our sin has on us?
4. How might we justify the assertion that sin is the root cause of all the problems we have in our relationships with other people?

PART THREE:

WHAT CHRIST HAS DONE

Chapter 7

THE DEATH
OF CHRIST

Christianity is a rescue religion. It declares that God has taken the initiative in Jesus Christ to rescue us from our sins. This is the main theme of the Bible.

> You are to give him the name Jesus, because he will save his people from their sins.

> The Son of Man came to seek and to save what was lost.

> Here is a trustworthy saying that deserves full acceptance: Christ Jesus came into the world to save sinners.

> We have seen and testify that the Father has sent his Son to be the Saviour of the world.[1]

More particularly, since, as we have seen, sin has three principal consequences, 'salvation' is about our liberation from them all. Through Jesus Christ the Saviour we can be brought out of

exile and put right with God; we can be born again, receive a
new nature and be set free from our moral bondage; and we can
have the old discords replaced by a harmony of love. Christ
made the first aspect of salvation possible by his suffering and
death, the second by the gift of his Spirit and the third by the
building of his church. The first will be our theme in this
chapter; the second and third in the next.

Paul described his work as a 'ministry of reconciliation' and
his gospel as a 'message of reconciliation'. He also made it quite
clear where this reconciliation comes from. God is its author,
he says, and Christ is the one through whom he brings it about.
'All this is from God, who reconciled us to himself through
Christ.' Again, 'God was reconciling the world to himself
in Christ.' Everything that was achieved through the death of
Jesus on the cross had its origin in the mind and heart of the
eternal God. No explanation of Christ's death or humanity's
salvation which downplays this fact does justice to the teaching
of the Bible. 'God so loved the world that he gave his one and
only Son, that whoever believes in him shall not perish but
have eternal life.' Again, 'God was pleased to have all his fulness
dwell in him, and through him to reconcile to himself all
things, whether things on earth or things in heaven, by making
peace through his blood, shed on the cross.'[2]

But what does this 'reconciliation' mean? The answer is that
it indicates either an action by which two parties in conflict are
brought together, or the state in which their oneness is enjoyed
and expressed. Paul says that this reconciliation is something
that we have received through our Lord and Saviour Jesus
Christ. We have not achieved it by our own efforts; we have
received it from him as a gift. Sin caused a separation between
us and God; the cross, the crucifixion of Christ, has brought us
back together. Sin made us enemies; the cross has brought

peace. Sin created a gulf between us and God; the cross has bridged it. Sin broke the relationship; the cross has restored it. To put the same truth across in different words, as Paul does in this letter to the Romans, 'The wages of sin is death, but the gift of God is eternal life in Christ Jesus our Lord.'

But why was the cross necessary for our salvation? Is it really vital to Christianity? What exactly did it achieve? We must now go on to consider the centrality and meaning of the cross.

THE CENTRALITY OF THE CROSS

In order to grasp that the death of Jesus as a sacrifice for sin is central to the message of the Bible, we must first go back to the Old Testament. Old Testament religion was sacrificial right from the start. Ever since Abel brought lambs from his flock and 'the LORD looked with favour on Abel and his offering', the worship of God involved bringing sacrifices to him. Altars were built, animals were killed and blood was shed long before the laws of Moses. But, under Moses, after the covenant between God and the people had been endorsed at Mount Sinai, what had been somewhat haphazard was regularized under God's law.

The great prophets of the eighth and seventh centuries BC protested against what they saw as the formalism and immorality of the worshippers, but the sacrificial system continued without interruption until the destruction of the temple in Jerusalem in AD 70. Every Jew was familiar with the rituals attached to the different offerings, as well as with the special occasions, daily, weekly, monthly and yearly when they had to be offered. No Jew could have failed to learn the fundamental lessons in all this process of education that 'the life of a creature is in the blood' and that 'without the shedding of blood there is no forgiveness'.[3]

The Old Testament sacrifices are a visible symbol which
points forward to the sacrifice of Christ. The prophets and
psalmists foretold it in words. We can see the death of Jesus
foreshadowed in the persecuted but innocent victim described
in certain psalms which were later applied to him. We detect
him in Zechariah's shepherd who is stricken and whose sheep
are scattered, and in Daniel's prince or 'Anointed One' who is
'cut off'. Above all, we can find him in the noble figure who
appears in the Servant Songs towards the end of the prophecy
of Isaiah, the suffering servant of the Lord, the despised 'man of
sorrows', who is punished for the transgressions of others, is led
like a lamb to the slaughter and bears the sin of many. As Jesus
himself explained to his disciples, 'This is what is written: The
Christ will suffer.'[4]

When Jesus came, he knew that he had a clear destination to
get to. He recognized that the Scriptures were pointing to him
and that their expectation was to be fulfilled in him. This is
particularly clear at the points which refer to his coming
sufferings. The turning point of his ministry came at Caesarea
Philippi when, immediately after Simon Peter had confessed
him to be the Christ, he 'began to teach them that the Son of
Man must suffer many things'.

It is this 'must', this sense of compulsion laid upon him by
the Scriptures, that revealed the Father's will, which constantly
recurs in his teaching. He had 'a baptism to undergo' and felt
himself constrained until the job was done. He kept moving
steadily towards the time of his death, which in the Gospel
accounts is said at several points not to have come just yet, until
at last, shortly before his arrest, with the cross in sight, he could
say, 'Father, the time has come.'

The prospect of the ordeal before him filled him with
apprehension. 'Now my heart is troubled, and what shall I say?

"Father, save me from this hour"? No, it was for this very reason I came to this hour. Father, glorify your name!' When the moment of his arrest finally arrived, and Simon lunged out with his sword to protect him, slashing the ear of the high priest's servant, Jesus rebuked him, 'Put your sword away! Shall I not drink the cup the Father has given me?' According to Matthew, Jesus added, 'Do you think I cannot call on my Father, and he will at once put at my disposal more than twelve legions of angels? But how then would the Scriptures be fulfilled that say it must happen in this way?'[5]

The supreme importance of the cross which the Old Testament foretold and Jesus taught is fully recognized by the New Testament authors. The writers of the four Gospels devote a disproportionate amount of space to Christ's last week and death when compared to the rest of his life and ministry: 40% of the first Gospel, 60% of the second, 33% of the third, and almost 50% of the fourth are given to an account of the events between his final entry into Jerusalem and his return to heaven. It is particularly striking in the case of John, whose Gospel has sometimes been divided into two equal halves which have been entitled 'The Book of the Signs' and 'The Book of the Passion'.

What is implied in the Gospels is stated explicitly in the New Testament's letters, most notably by Paul, who never grew tired of reminding his readers about the cross. He himself expressed a vivid sense of gratitude to the Saviour who had died for him. 'The Son of God ... loved me', he could write, 'and gave himself for me', and therefore, 'May I never boast except in the cross of our Lord Jesus Christ.'

To the Corinthians, who were in danger of being tangled up in the subtleties of Greek philosophy, Paul wrote, 'Jews demand miraculous signs and Greeks look for wisdom, but we preach Christ crucified: a stumbling-block to Jews and foolishness to Gentiles, but to those whom God has called, both Jews and Greeks, Christ the power of God and the wisdom of God.' This was what he had in fact asserted when he first came to Corinth from Athens on his second missionary journey: 'I resolved to know nothing while I was with you except Jesus Christ and him crucified,' and again, 'What I received I passed on to you as of first importance: that Christ died for our sins according to the Scriptures.'[6]

The same emphasis on the cross is to be found in the rest of the New Testament. What Peter thought and wrote about it we shall see later. In the epistle to the Hebrews comes the clear statement that Christ 'has appeared once for all at the culmination of the ages to do away with sin by the sacrifice of himself'. When we reach the mysterious and wonderful book of Revelation, we catch a glimpse of the glorified Jesus in heaven not only as 'the Lion of the tribe of Judah', but as 'a Lamb, looking as if it had been slain', and we hear the countless multitude of saints and angels singing his praise, 'Worthy is the Lamb, who was slain, to receive power and wealth and wisdom and strength and honour and glory and praise!'[7]

So from the early chapters of Genesis to the final chapters of Revelation we can see what some writers have called a 'scarlet thread', which enables us to trace our route on the map that is the Bible. What the Bible teaches concerning the centrality of the cross has been recognized and celebrated by the Christian church from the very beginning. Many churches mark new members with the sign of a cross at their baptism and erect crosses over the graves of those who have died. Church buildings have often been constructed on a cross-shaped ground plan, with nave and transepts forming a cross, while many Christians wear a cross on lapel, necklace or chain. None of this is accidental. The cross is the symbol of our faith. The Christian faith is 'the faith of Christ crucified'. There is no Christianity without the cross. But why? What does it mean?

THE MEANING OF THE CROSS

I cannot begin to unfold the meaning of the death of Christ without first admitting that much remains a mystery. Christians believe that the cross is the pivotal event in history. Little wonder that our tiny minds cannot fully take it in! One day the veil will be altogether removed, and all will become clear. We shall see Christ as he is and worship him through eternity for what he has done. 'Now we see only a reflection as in a mirror; then we shall see face to face. Now I know in part; then I shall know fully, even as I am fully known' (TNIV). So wrote the great apostle Paul with his massive intellect and his many profound insights; and if he said it, how much more should we?

I have deliberately chosen to limit myself here to what Simon Peter wrote about the death of Jesus in his first New Testament letter. I have three reasons.

The first reason is that Peter was one of the inner core of three apostles. 'Peter, James and John' form a trio who enjoyed a closer relationship with Jesus than the other disciples. So Peter is as likely as anyone to have grasped what Jesus thought and taught concerning his death. In fact, we find in his first letter several clear recollections of his Master's teaching.

Secondly, I turn to Peter with confidence, because at the beginning he was himself very reluctant to accept that Christ had to suffer in the way that he did. He had been the first to acknowledge the uniqueness of who Christ was, but he was also the first to deny the need for his death. He who had declared, 'You are the Messiah,' shouted, 'Never, Lord!' when Jesus began to teach that the Christ must suffer. Throughout the remaining days of Jesus' ministry, Peter held on in his dogged hostility to the idea of a Christ who would die. He tried to prevent Jesus from being arrested, and, even after this proved futile, followed him at a distance. In sullen disappointment, he denied three times that he even knew him, and the tears he wept were tears of shame, yes, but also despair. Only after the resurrection, when Jesus taught the apostles from the Bible that it was 'necessary that the Christ should suffer these things and enter into his glory', did Simon Peter at last begin to understand and believe. Within a few weeks he had grasped the truth so firmly that he could address the crowd in the temple cloisters with the words, 'God fulfilled what he had foretold through all the prophets, saying that his Messiah would suffer', and his first letter contains several references to Christ's sufferings and glory. We too may at first be reluctant to admit that the cross was necessary and slow to understand its meaning, but if anyone can persuade and teach us it will be Simon Peter.

Thirdly, the references to the cross in Peter's first letter are asides. If he were deliberately gathering arguments to prove that the death of Jesus was essential, we might suspect him of having some axe to grind. But his references to it are more about behaviour than belief. He simply urges his readers to live their Christian lives consistently and to put up with their sufferings patiently, and then refers them to the cross for their inspiration.

Christ died as our Example

Persecution is the background to this letter. The Emperor Nero was known to be hostile to the Christian church, and many Christians feared for their future. There had already been spasmodic outbreaks of violence and it looked as though worse was to come.

The advice Peter gives is straightforward.[8] If Christian servants are being treated badly by their pagan masters, let them make sure that they are not receiving a punishment which they deserve. It is no credit to them to accept a beating for doing wrong. Let them rather suffer for the sake of what is right and welcome criticism for the name of Christ. They are not to resist, still less to take revenge. They must submit. To bear unjust suffering patiently brings God's approval. Then at once Peter's mind flies to the cross. Undeserved suffering is part of the Christian's calling, he asserts, 'because Christ suffered for you, leaving you an example, that you should follow in his steps'. He was without sin or deceit. When he was insulted, he chose not to retaliate; he didn't issue any threats when he suffered. He simply committed his tormentors into the hands of the just Judge of all humanity.

Christ has left us an example. The Greek word Peter uses, unique here in the New Testament, denotes a teacher's copybook, the perfect alphabet on which a pupil models his script as he learns to write. So if we want to master the ABC of Christian love, we must trace out our lives according to the pattern of Jesus. We must 'follow in his steps'. Coming from Peter's pen, the use of this verb is all the more striking. He had boasted that he would follow Jesus to prison and to death, but in the event had 'followed him at a distance'. But then, after the resurrection, Jesus renewed his call and commission to Peter in his familiar terms, 'Follow me.' So Peter was urging his readers to join him as he tried now to follow more obediently in the Master's steps.

The challenge of the cross is as uncomfortable now as it was then, and is as relevant today as it has ever been. Perhaps nothing is more completely opposed to our natural instincts than this command not to resist, but to bear unjust suffering and overcome evil with good. Yet the cross urges us to accept injury, love our enemies and leave the outcome to God.

But the death of Jesus is more than an inspiring example. If this were all there is to it, much of what we find in the Gospels would make no sense. There are those strange sayings, for instance, in which Jesus said he would 'give his life as a ransom for many' and shed his blood – 'blood of the covenant', he called it – 'for the forgiveness of sins'.[9] There is no redemption in an example. A pattern cannot secure our pardon.

Besides, why was he weighed down with such heavy and anxious apprehension as the cross approached? How shall we explain the dreadful agony in the garden, his tears and cries and bloody sweat? 'My Father, if it is possible, may this cup be taken from me. Yet not as I will, but as you will.' Again, 'My Father, if it is not possible for this cup to be taken away unless I drink it, may your will be done.' Was the 'cup' which he hesitated to drink from the symbol of death by crucifixion? Was he then afraid of pain and death? If so, his example may have been one of submission and patience, but it was hardly one of courage. Plato tells us that Socrates drank his cup of hemlock in the prison cell in Athens 'quite readily and cheerfully'. Was Socrates braver than Jesus? Or is it that their cups contained different poisons? And what is the meaning of the darkness, and the cry of abandonment, and the tearing from top to bottom of the temple curtain in front of the Holy of Holies? There is no way of understanding these things if Jesus died only as an example. Indeed, some of them would seem to make his example less commendable.

Not only would much in the Gospels remain mysterious if Christ's death were purely an example, but our human need would remain unsatisfied. We need more than an example; we need a Saviour. An example can stir our imagination, kindle our idealism and strengthen our resolve, but it cannot remove the stains of our past sins, bring peace to our troubled conscience, or restore our relationship with God.

In any case, the apostles leave us in no doubt about the matter. They repeatedly associate Christ's coming and death with our *sins*.

> Christ died for our sins according to the Scriptures.

> Christ ... suffered once for sins, the righteous for the unrighteous, to bring you to God.

> You know that he appeared so that he might take away our sins.

Here are the three great writers of the New Testament, the apostles Paul, Peter and John, unanimous in linking his death with our sins.[10]

Christ died as our Sinbearer

In his letter (2:24 TNIV), the way Peter describes the relationship between Christ's death and our sins is this: 'He himself bore our sins in his body on the cross.' The expression 'to bear sin' sounds rather strange to us, and we shall need to go back to the Old Testament to understand it. The idea occurs frequently in the books of Leviticus and Numbers. It is emphasized many times that those who break God's laws bear the responsibility for their actions. For instance, 'If anyone sins and does what is forbidden in any of the LORD's commands ... they are guilty and will be held responsible.'[11]

But at times it is implied that somebody else can assume responsibility for the wrongdoer. In Numbers 30, which deals with the validity of vows, Moses explains that a vow taken by a man or a widow must stand. But a vow taken by an unmarried girl or by a married woman must be confirmed by her father or her husband respectively. If, when the man hears of the woman's vow, he says nothing to nullify it, and it later proves to have been foolish, it is said that '*he* must bear the consequences of *her* wrongdoing'. Another example comes towards the end of the book of Lamentations, in which after the destruction of Jerusalem the Israelites cry: 'Our parents sinned and are no more; and *we* bear *their* punishment.'

This possibility of somebody else accepting the responsibility for, and bearing the consequences of, our sins was further taught by those Old Testament blood sacrifices in the laws of Moses which seem so strange to us today. Leviticus 10 tells us God made provision for the sin offering to 'take away the guilt of the community by making atonement for them before the LORD'. Similarly, on the annual Day of Atonement, Aaron was told to lay his hands on the head of the animal chosen to be what we call the 'scapegoat'. In this way he identified himself and the people with it; he was then to confess the nation's sins, symbolically transferring them to the goat, which was driven out into the desert. We then read that 'the goat will carry on itself all their sins to a solitary place'.[12] It is clear from this that to 'bear' somebody else's sin is to become their substitute, to take responsibility for the penalty of their sin in their place.

But all this was only a temporary provision. For, as the writer to the Hebrews says, 'it is impossible for the blood of bulls and goats to take away sins'. So in the longest Servant Song of Isaiah (chapter 53), the innocent sufferer (who signifies the coming Christ) is very deliberately described using the language of sacrifice. He was 'led like a lamb to the slaughter', both because 'he did not open his mouth' and because 'the

LORD has laid on him the iniquity of us all', so that his life was made 'a guilt offering'. 'We all, like sheep, have gone astray', but he also, like a sheep, 'was pierced for our transgressions, he was crushed for our iniquities; the punishment that brought us peace was upon him, and by his wounds we are healed'. All this clear language of substitution, describing him as 'stricken' for 'the transgression of my people', is summed up in the chapter in the two phrases which we have already reflected on: 'he will bear their iniquities' and 'he bore the sin of many'.

When at last, after centuries of preparation, Jesus Christ himself arrived, John the Baptist greeted him publicly with the extraordinary words: 'Look, the Lamb of God, who takes away the sin of the world!' Similarly, when later the New Testament came to be written, its authors had no difficulty in seeing the death of Jesus as the one final sacrifice in which all the Old Testament sacrifices were fulfilled. This truth is an important part of the message of the letter to the Hebrews. The old sacrifices were of bulls and goats: Christ offered himself. The old sacrifices were repeated over and over again: Christ died once and for all. He was 'sacrificed once to take away the sins of many people'.

This last phrase brings us back to Peter's expression, 'he himself bore our sins in his body on the cross'. The Son of God identified himself with the sins of humanity. He was not content just to take our nature on himself; he took our sins on himself as well. He not only 'became flesh' in the womb of Mary; he was 'made to be sin' on the cross on which he died.

This last phrase is from Paul and is perhaps the most startling statement that the Bible makes about the death of Jesus. But we cannot escape its significance. In the previous verses (in 2 Corinthians 5) Paul has affirmed that God refused to count our sins against us. In his completely undeserved love for us, he decided not to make us answerable for our sins. He would not allow it to be said of us (as it was said of so many in Old Testament times) that 'they will be held responsible'. So what did he do? 'God made him who had no sin to be sin for us, so that in him we might become the righteousness of God.' Jesus Christ had no sins of his own; he was made sin with our sins, on the cross.

As we reflect on the cross, we can begin to understand the terrible implications of these words. At twelve noon 'darkness came over the whole land', which continued for three hours until Jesus died. With the darkness came silence, for no eye should see, and no lips could tell, the agony of soul which the spotless Lamb of God was now enduring. The accumulated sins from the whole of human history were laid upon him. Voluntarily he bore them in his own body. He made them his own. He took full responsibility for them.

The accumulated sins from the whole of human history were laid upon him.

And then, in desolate spiritual abandonment, a cry was wrung from his lips, 'My God, my God, why have you forsaken me?' It was a quotation from the first verse of Psalm 22. He had probably been reflecting during his agony on its description of the sufferings and glory of the Messiah. But why did he quote that particular verse? Why not one of the triumphant verses at the end? Why not, 'You who fear the Lord, praise him!' or 'Dominion belongs to the Lord'? Are we driven to conclude that it was a cry of human weakness and despair, or that the Son of God was imagining things?

No. These words must be taken at face value. He quoted this verse from the Bible, as he had quoted so many others, because he believed that he himself was fulfilling it. He was bearing our sins. And God, whose 'eyes are too pure to look on evil' and who 'cannot tolerate wrong', turned his face away. Our sins came between the Father and the Son. The Lord Jesus Christ, who was eternally with the Father, who enjoyed unbroken communion with him throughout his life on earth, was momentarily abandoned. Our sins sent Christ to hell. He tasted the agony of a soul alienated from God. Bearing our sins, he died our death. He endured instead of us the penalty of separation from God which our sins deserved.

Then at once, emerging from that outer darkness, he cried out in triumph, 'It is finished,' and finally, 'Father, into your hands I commit my spirit.' And so he died. The work he had come to do was completed. The salvation he had come to win was accomplished. The sins of the world had been carried away. Reconciliation to God was available to all who would trust this Saviour for themselves, and receive him as their own. Immediately, as if to demonstrate this truth publicly, the unseen hand of God tore down the curtain in the temple. It was no longer needed. The way into God's holy presence was no longer barred. Christ had 'opened the gate of heaven to all believers'. And thirty-six hours later he was raised from the dead, to prove that he had not died in vain.

This simple and wonderful account of the sinbearing of the Son of God is strangely unpopular today. The idea that he should have borne our sins and taken our penalty is said to be immoral or unworthy or unjust. And of course it can easily be distorted and made a mockery of. We are not suggesting that there is nothing left for us to do. Of course we must return 'to the Shepherd and Overseer of our souls', dying to sin and living to righteousness, as Peter went on to say. Above all, we must not forget that 'all this is from God' and that it springs from his unimaginable mercy. We are not to think of Jesus Christ as a third party wresting salvation for us from a God who is unwilling to save. No. The initiative lay with God himself. 'God was reconciling the world to himself in Christ.' Precisely *how* he can have been in Christ while at the same time making Christ to be sin for us, I cannot explain, but the apostle states both truths in the same paragraph without any awkwardness. This is one of the paradoxes of the Christian faith – to be accepted along with the equally baffling paradox that the evidence points to Jesus of Nazareth being both God and Man, and yet one person. If there is a paradox in who he was, it should come as no surprise that there is one in what he did as well.

But even if we are unable to resolve the paradox or fully understand the mystery, we can still rely on the direct statements of Christ and his apostles. Their united testimony is that he bore our sins, a phrase whose meaning in the Bible is that he paid the penalty of our sins for us.

Three considerations make it clear that this is indeed what Peter meant. First, there is one of his early addresses recorded in the Acts, in which he said, 'The God of our fathers raised Jesus from the dead – whom you had killed by hanging him on a tree.' His Jewish listeners would have had no difficulty in grasping the implied reference to Deuteronomy 21, which indicates that 'anyone who is hung on a tree is under God's curse'. The fact that Jesus ended his life hanging on a 'tree' (for the Jews regarded being nailed to a cross as equivalent to being hanged on a tree) meant that he was cursed by God.

Instead of roundly rejecting this idea, the apostles accepted it, and Paul explained it in Galatians 3. He pointed out that

Deuteronomy also says: 'Cursed is anyone who does not uphold the words of this law by carrying them out' (TNIV). But then 'Christ redeemed us from the curse of the law by becoming a curse for us, for it is written: "Cursed is everyone who is hung on a tree."' What these verses mean in the context is plain and inescapable. It is this: the fully justified curse which rests on those who break God's law was transferred to Jesus on the cross. He has set us free from this curse by taking it upon himself when he died.

Secondly, this passage in Peter's first letter contains no fewer than five clear references back to Isaiah 53:

1 Peter 2	Isaiah 53
He committed no sin, and no deceit was found in his mouth	He had done no violence, nor was any deceit in his mouth
They hurled their insults at him	He was despised and rejected
He himself bore our sins	He bore the sin of many
By his wounds you have been healed	By his wounds we are healed
You were like sheep going astray	We all, like sheep, have gone astray

We have already seen that this chapter portrays an innocent sufferer who is wounded for the transgressions of others in a sacrificial death. There is no doubt that Jesus himself interpreted his mission and death in the light of this chapter, as did his followers after him. For example, in Acts 8, when the Ethiopian official asked the evangelist Philip to whom the prophet was referring in this passage which he was reading in his chariot, Philip immediately 'told him the good news of Jesus'.

Thirdly, Peter makes other references to the cross in this

letter which confirm what we have already seen from chapter 2. He describes his readers as having been 'redeemed ... with the precious blood of Christ, a lamb without blemish or defect' and even as having been 'chosen' for 'sprinkling' with his blood.[13] Both expressions look back to the original Passover sacrifice at the time of the Old Testament exodus. Each Israelite family was to take a lamb, kill it, and sprinkle its blood on the door frame of their house. Only those who did this were safe from the judgment of God and escaped from the slavery of Egypt. Peter boldly applies this symbolism to Christ (as also does Paul, 'Christ, our Passover lamb, has been sacrificed'). His blood was shed to rescue us from the judgment of God and the tyranny of sin. If we are to benefit from it, it must be 'sprinkled' on our hearts, that is, applied to each of us individually.

Peter's other significant reference to the cross is in 3:18: 'Christ also suffered once for sins, the righteous for the unrighteous, to bring you to God' (TNIV). Sin had separated us from God; but Christ wanted to bring us back to God. So he suffered for our sins, an innocent Saviour dying for guilty sinners. And he did it just the 'once', decisively, so that what he did cannot be repeated or improved upon or even supplemented.

We must not miss what this implies. It means that no religious observance or good behaviour on our part could ever earn our forgiveness. Yet a great many people accept the caricature of Christianity which claims that we can. They see religion as a system of human merit. 'God helps those who help themselves,' they say. But there is no way that this view can be reconciled with the cross of Christ. He died to take away our sins for the simple reason that we cannot remove them ourselves. If we could, his atoning death would be unnecessary.

Indeed, to claim that we can end up in God's good books by our own efforts is an insult to Jesus Christ. It is equivalent to saying that we can manage without him and that he really need not have bothered to die. As Paul put it, 'If righteousness [i.e. being put right with God] could be gained through the law [i.e. through us keeping the rules], Christ died for nothing!'[14]

The message of the cross remains, in our day as in Paul's, foolishness to the wise and a stumbling-block to the self-righteous, but it has brought peace to the conscience of millions. There is healing through the wounds of Christ, life through his death, pardon through his pain, salvation through his suffering.

STUDY QUESTIONS

1. How does salvation set us free from the 'three principal consequences' of sin?
2. Why was it necessary for Jesus to die on the cross in order for sins to be forgiven?
3. How does the teaching of the Old Testament help us to understand the significance of the cross?
4. Under what circumstances does the death of Jesus provide us with an example to follow?
5. Why is it so important to see the death of Jesus as so much 'more than an inspiring example'?
6. 'We are not to think of Jesus Christ as a third party wresting salvation for us from a God who is unwilling to save.' Why might people think this? What is it that helps to correct such a view?
7. How does the death of Jesus underline the impossibility of the claim that 'we can end up in God's good books by our own efforts'?

Chapter 8

THE SALVATION
OF CHRIST

'Salvation' is a wonderfully wide-ranging word and it would be a great mistake to think that it refers only to the forgiveness of our sins. God is as much concerned with our present and future as with our past. His plan is first to put right our relationship with him, and then progressively to set us free from our self-centredness and bring us into harmony with other people. We owe our forgiveness and reconciliation chiefly to the death of Christ, but it is by his Spirit that we can be set free from ourselves and in his church that we can be united in a fellowship of love. These are the aspects of Christ's salvation to which we now turn.

THE SPIRIT OF CHRIST
As we have seen, we should not view our sins as a series of unrelated incidents, but as the symptoms of an inner moral disease. To illustrate this, Jesus used the picture of the fruit tree. The quality of fruit, he taught, depends on the quality of the tree from which it comes. 'Every good tree bears good fruit,

but a bad tree bears bad fruit. A good tree cannot bear bad fruit, and a bad tree cannot bear good fruit.'

The cause of our sins, therefore, is our sin, our inherited nature, which is polluted and self-centred. As Jesus put it, our sins come from within, out of our 'heart'. This is why an improvement in behaviour depends on a change of nature. 'Make the tree good,' said Jesus, 'and its fruit will be good.'

But can human nature be changed? Is it possible to make a sour person sweet, a proud person humble, or a selfish person unselfish? The Bible declares emphatically that these miracles can take place. It is part of the wonder of the gospel. Jesus Christ offers to change not only our standing before God, but our very nature. He spoke to Nicodemus about the crucial need for a new birth, and his words still apply to us today: 'Very truly I tell you, no-one can see the kingdom of God without being born again ... You should not be surprised at my saying, "You must be born again."' [1]

In some respects, the way Paul puts it is even more dramatic. He blurts out a sentence which, in its original Greek, has no verbs: 'If anyone in Christ – new creation!' [2] This, then, is the possibility of which the New Testament speaks – a new heart, a new nature, a new birth, a new creation.

This amazing inner change is the work of the Holy Spirit. The new birth is a birth 'from above'. To be born again is to be 'born of the Spirit'. We don't need at this point to go into the intricacies of what Christians believe about the Trinity. For the time being, it is enough simply to consider what the apostles had to say about the Holy Spirit as they reflected on their experience of what had happened to them.

First, however, it is important to realize that the Holy Spirit didn't suddenly come into existence at the point when the disciples began to experience him on the Day of Pentecost, a few days after Jesus returned to heaven. The Holy Spirit is God. He has always existed and has been at work in the world right from the very beginning. The Old Testament contains many references to him, and the prophets looked forward to the time when his activity would increase and spread, when God would put his Spirit within his people, and so enable them to live in obedience to him.

While the Old Testament prophets indicated that this would happen at some unspecified time in the future, Christ promised that the Spirit would come like this very soon. A few hours before he died, he met with his disciples in an upstairs room and talked about 'the Advocate', 'the Spirit of truth', who would come and take his place.

Indeed, the presence of the Holy Spirit would be even better for them than his own presence on earth had been. 'It is for your good that I am going away,' he said. 'Unless I go away, the Advocate will not come to you; but if I go, I will send him to you.' The advantage was that Christ had only been *with* them, at their side; but 'he ... will be *in* you'.[3]

There is a sense in which we may say that the teaching ministry of Jesus was a failure. Several times he had urged his disciples to humble themselves like little children, but Simon Peter remained proud and self-confident. He had often told them to love one another, but even John seems to have deserved his nickname 'son of thunder' right up to the end. Yet when we read Peter's first letter, we cannot fail to notice its references to humility, and John's letters are full of love. What made the difference? The Holy Spirit. Jesus taught them to be humble and loving; but neither quality appeared in their lives until the Holy Spirit entered their personalities and began to change them from the inside.

The second chapter of the book of Acts tells us about the

Day of Pentecost and how 'all of them were filled with the Holy Spirit'. We shouldn't imagine that this was a freak experience just for them, although we are not to expect an exact repetition of some of the things that happened then, like the rushing wind and tongues of fire. But 'be filled with the Spirit' is a command addressed to all Christians. The inner presence of the Holy Spirit is a spiritual legacy for every Christian. Indeed, if the Holy Spirit has not made his home within us, we are not real Christians at all. As Paul wrote, 'If anyone does not have the Spirit of Christ, they do not belong to Christ.'[4]

This, then, is what the New Testament teaches. When we put our trust in Jesus Christ and commit ourselves to him, the Holy Spirit enters us. He is sent by God 'into our hearts'. He makes our bodies his dwelling place, his temple.[5]

This does not mean that we are no longer able to sin. Not a bit of it! Indeed, in some ways the conflict intensifies; but on the other hand, a way of victory has been opened. Paul gives a vivid description of the battle in the fifth chapter of his letter to the Galatians. The opponents fighting it out are 'the sinful nature' and 'the Spirit'. 'The sinful nature', he explains, 'desires what is contrary to the Spirit, and the Spirit what is contrary to the sinful nature. They are in conflict with each other.'

This is not dry theological theory; it is the daily experience of every Christian. We continue to be aware of sinful desires which pull us down; but we are now also aware of a counter-acting force which is drawing us upwards to holiness. If we allowed the sinful nature to have free rein, it would stampede us into the jungle of immorality and selfishness which Paul lists in verses 19–21. If, on the other hand, the Holy Spirit is allowed his way, the result will be 'love, joy, peace, patience, kindness, goodness, faithfulness, gentleness and self-control'.

Paul calls these attractive qualities 'the fruit of the Spirit'. He pictures our human character as an orchard which the Holy Spirit is cultivating. Let him make the trees good, and their fruit will be good too.

How, then, can the sinful nature be subdued, so that the fruit of the Spirit may grow and ripen? The answer lies in our attitude to it. 'Those who belong to Christ Jesus have crucified the sinful nature with its passions and desires.' 'Live by [or 'in'] the Spirit, and you will not gratify the desires of the sinful nature.' We must take up an attitude of such fierce resistance and ruthless rejection towards the sinful nature that only the word 'crucifixion' will do to describe it; but we must surrender the undisputed authority over our lives to the Spirit who lives within us. The more we make a habit of saying 'no' to the sinful nature and 'yes' to the Spirit, the more the ugly works of the flesh will disappear and the delightful fruit of the Spirit will take their place.

Paul teaches the same truth in 2 Corinthians 3:18: 'We, who with unveiled faces all reflect the Lord's glory, are being transformed into his likeness with ever-increasing glory, which comes from the Lord, who is the Spirit.' It is by the Spirit of Christ that we can be changed so that we become more like Christ, as we continue to maintain our focus on him. Yes, we have our part to play, in turning from what we know to be wrong, in the exercise of faith and discipline. But making us holy is essentially the work of the Holy Spirit.

William Temple used to illustrate the point in this way. It is no good giving me a play like *Hamlet* or *King Lear*, and telling me to write a new play just like it. Shakespeare could do it; I can't. And it is no good showing me a life like the life of Jesus and telling me to live a life just like it. Jesus could do it; I can't. But if the genius of Shakespeare could come and live inside me,

I would then be able to write plays like he did. And if the Spirit of Jesus could come and live inside me, I would then be able to live a life like he did. This is the open secret of how to live as a Christian. It is not about us struggling in vain to become more like Jesus, but about allowing him, by the power of his Spirit, to come and change us from the inside. Once again we see that to have him as our example is not enough; we need him as our Saviour.

It is through his death on the cross that the penalty of our sins may be forgiven; it is through his Spirit making his home within us that the power of our sins may be overcome.

THE CHURCH OF CHRIST

Sin tends to pull us out of harmony with other people. It alienates us not only from our Creator, but also from our fellow creatures. We all know from experience how easily a community, whether a college, a hospital, a factory or an office, can become a hotbed of jealousy and ill feeling. We find it very difficult 'to live together in unity'.

But God's plan is to restore our relationships with one another as well as with himself. So he does not save independent, unconnected individuals in isolation from one another; he is calling out *a people* to belong to him.

This is made clear right from the start in the early chapters of Genesis. God called Abraham to leave his home and relations in Mesopotamia, and promised to give him both a land for his inheritance and descendants as numerous as the stars in the sky and the grains of sand on the beach. This promise to multiply Abraham's offspring and through them to bless all the nations of the earth was renewed to his son Isaac and his grandson Jacob.

Although Jacob died in exile in Egypt, his twelve sons survived him and became the ancestors of the twelve tribes of

'Israel', the new name God had given to Jacob. It was with these 'children of Israel', rescued years later from their Egyptian slavery, that God renewed the promises he had made to Abraham.

But how exactly were all the families of the earth to be blessed? As the centuries rolled by and the history of God's people unfolded, it seemed to the rest of the world that Israel was more of a curse than a blessing. God's people built high walls around them to protect themselves from being contaminated by contact with the Gentiles. It looked as though they were going to miss out on God's plan for them to bless the other nations of the world. So had God's promise to Abraham been completely hollow? No. The predictions of many of the prophets pointed to the time when the Messiah would appear. That's when, at last, people from every point of the compass would come and enter the kingdom of God.

At last the Messiah came. Jesus of Nazareth announced the arrival of the global kingdom which had been anticipated for such a long time. Many would come, he said, from north, south, east and west, and sit down with Abraham, Isaac and Jacob. God's people would no longer be isolated, but a society whose members would be drawn from every nation on earth. 'Go . . .' the risen Jesus told his followers, 'and make disciples of all nations.' The sum total of these disciples he called 'my church'.[6]

So God's undertaking to Abraham, repeated several times to him and renewed to his sons, is being fulfilled in the growth of the worldwide church today. 'If you belong to Christ,' wrote Paul, 'then you are Abraham's seed, and heirs according to the promise.'[7]

One of the most striking pictures which Paul uses to express the unity of believers in Christ is that of the human body. The church, he says, is the body of Christ. Every Christian is a member or organ of the body, while Christ himself is the head, controlling the body's activities. Not every organ has the same function, but each is necessary for the maximum health and usefulness of the body.

The whole body is also energized by a common life. This is the Holy Spirit. It is his presence which makes the body one. The church owes its unity to him. 'There is one body and one Spirit,' emphasizes Paul. Even the divisions in the outward organization of the church, regrettable as they are, do not destroy its inward and spiritual unity. This is unbreakable, since it is 'the unity of the Spirit' or 'the fellowship of the Spirit'.[8] It is our common share in him which makes us deeply and permanently one.

It would, of course, be ridiculous to claim to belong to a great worldwide body, the church universal, without in practice sharing in one of its local expressions. It is here, as members of a local church, that we find opportunities to worship God, to enjoy fellowship with one another and to serve the wider community.

Many today react against the church as an institution, and some entirely reject it. This is often understandable, for the church can certainly be desperately old-fashioned and inward-looking. We need to remember, though, that the church is made up of people – sinful and fallible people. This is no reason to reject it, for all of us are sinful and fallible too.

We also have to bear in mind that not everyone who belongs to the visible church is necessarily a member of the real church of Jesus Christ. Some whose names are included on church rolls and registers have never had their names, as Jesus put it, 'written in heaven'. Although this is a fact to which the Bible often refers, it is not for us to judge, for 'the Lord knows those who are his'.

Those who *declare* faith in Christ are welcomed into the visible church through being baptized. But only God knows those who actually *exercise* faith, for only he can see the heart. There is certainly a considerable overlap between the two groups. But they are not identical.

The Holy Spirit is not only the author of the common life of the church, but is also the creator of its common love. The chief fruit of the Spirit is love. His very nature is love, and he gives it to those in whom he dwells. All Christians have shared the remarkable experience of being drawn to other Christians whom they hardly know and whose background may be very different from their own. The relationship which exists and grows between the children of God is deeper and more special even than blood relationships. It is the life of the family of God in action. The truth is that 'we know that we have passed from death to life, because we love each other', as John says. This love is not sentimental nor even necessarily emotional. Its essence is self-sacrifice; it reveals itself in the desire to serve, help and enrich others. It is by love that the divisive force of sin is neutralized, for love unites where sin divides, and brings together where sin pulls apart.

It is by love that the divisive force of sin is neutralized, for love unites where sin divides, and brings together where sin pulls apart.

Of course, the pages of the church's history have often been spoiled by foolishness and selfishness, even by outright disobedience to the teaching of Christ. Still today some churches appear to be dead or dying, rather than vibrant with life; and others are torn by divisions and plagued with lovelessness. We have to admit that not all those who call themselves Christians show either the love or the life of Jesus Christ.

Even so, the Christian should be part of the local Christian community and be committed to sharing in its worship and witness, however imperfect it may be. For the church is the place where we find the new quality of relationship which Christ himself gives to those who belong to him.

STUDY QUESTIONS

1. The forgiveness of sins is wonderful enough – but what more is there to salvation?
2. How would you respond to someone who claimed that it is impossible to change human nature?
3. In what ways can we cooperate with the Holy Spirit in his work of transforming our lives?
4. What is the church? Why is it so important?

PART FOUR:

HOW TO RESPOND

Chapter 9

COUNTING
THE COST

So far we have looked at some of the evidence for the unique deity of Jesus of Nazareth; we have considered our need as sinners, alienated from God, imprisoned within ourselves and out of harmony with one another; and we have set out the main aspects of the salvation which Christ has won for us, and offers to us. It is now time for us to echo the very personal question put to Jesus Christ by Saul of Tarsus on the road to Damascus, 'What shall I do, Lord?' or the similar question asked by the jailer at Philippi, 'What must I do to be saved?'

Clearly we must do something. After all, Christianity is far more than accepting a series of statements about Jesus, true though they are. We may believe everything there is to believe about Christ, and admit that we are indeed sinners in need of his salvation, but this does not make us Christians. We have to make a personal response to Jesus Christ, committing ourselves totally to him as our Saviour and Lord. We shall consider exactly how we do this in the next chapter. Meanwhile, we shall look at some of the practical implications of what it means to be a Christian today.

Jesus never concealed the fact that his religion included a demand as well as an offer. Indeed, the demand was as total as the offer was free. His offer of salvation always brings with it the requirement that we obey him. He gave no encouragement at all to those who applied to become his disciples without thinking it through. He brought no pressure to bear on any enquirer. He sent irresponsible enthusiasts away with nothing. Luke tells us of three people who either volunteered, or were invited, to follow Jesus; but not one of them passed the Lord's tests. There was also the rich young ruler – an individual who was good, earnest and attractive in many ways, but who wanted eternal life on his own terms. He went away sad, with his wealth intact, but possessing neither eternal life nor Christ.

On another occasion, great crowds were following Jesus. Perhaps they were shouting out slogans of allegiance and giving an impressive outward display of their loyalty. But Jesus knew how superficial it all was. So he stopped and turned to speak to them, telling them a pointed parable in the form of a question:

> Suppose one of you wants to build a tower. Won't you first sit down and estimate the cost to see if you have enough money to complete it? For if you lay the foundation and are not able to finish it, everyone who sees it will ridicule you, saying, 'This person began to build and wasn't able to finish.'[1]

The Christian landscape is strewn with the wreckage of derelict, half-built towers – the ruins of those who began to build and were unable to finish. All too many people still ignore Christ's warning and undertake to follow him without first pausing to reflect on the cost of doing so. The result is the great scandal of so-called 'nominal Christianity'. In countries to which Christian civilization has spread, large numbers of people have covered themselves with a decent, but thin, veneer of Christianity. They have allowed themselves to become a little bit involved; enough to be respectable, but not enough to be uncomfortable. Their religion is a great, soft cushion. It protects them from the hard unpleasantness of life, while changing its place and shape to suit their convenience. No wonder cynics complain of hypocrites in the church and dismiss religion as escapism.

The message of Jesus was very different. He never lowered his standards or changed his conditions to make his call easier to accept. He asked his first disciples, and he has asked every disciple since, to give him their thoughtful and total commitment. Nothing less than this will do.

So let us look at precisely what he said.

He called the crowd to him along with his disciples and said: 'Whoever wants to be my disciple must deny themselves and take up their cross and follow me. For whoever wants to save their life will lose it, but whoever loses their life for me and for the gospel will save it. What good is it for you to gain the whole world, yet forfeit your soul? Or what can you give in exchange for your soul? If any of you are ashamed of me and my words in this adulterous and sinful generation, the Son of Man will be ashamed of you when he comes in his Father's glory with the holy angels.'[2]

THE CALL TO FOLLOW CHRIST

At its simplest, Christ's call was 'Follow me'. He asked men and women for their personal allegiance. He invited them to learn from him, to obey his words and to identify themselves with his cause.

Now there can be no following without a previous forsaking. To follow Christ is to give up all lesser loyalties. In the days of his ministry on earth, this often meant a literal abandonment of home and work. Simon and Andrew 'left their nets and followed him'. James and John 'left their father Zebedee in the boat with the hired men and followed him'. Matthew, who heard Christ's call while he was sitting at his tax booth, got up, left everything and followed him.

In principle, the call of the Lord Jesus is unchanged today. He still says, 'Follow me,' and adds, 'those of you who do not give up everything you have cannot be my disciple.' In practice, however, this does not mean for most Christians that they will need to move out of their home or leave their job. What it does imply, though, is the need for an inner surrender of these things, and a refusal to allow either family or ambition to occupy the first place in our lives.

Let me be more explicit about what needs to be abandoned, which cannot be separated from what it means to follow Jesus Christ.

First, there must be *a renunciation of sin*. The word for this is repentance and it is the first step in Christian conversion. There is no way round it. Repentance and faith belong together. We cannot follow Christ without forsaking sin.

Repentance is a definite turning away from every thought, word, deed and habit that we know to be wrong. It is not enough to feel pangs of remorse or to make some kind of apology to God. In essence, repentance is a matter neither of what we feel nor of what we say. It is an inward change of mind and attitude towards sin which leads to a change of behaviour.

There can be no compromise here. There may be sins in our lives which we do not think we could ever let go of; but we must be *willing* to let them go and ask God to deliver us from them. If you are unsure about what is right and what wrong, about what must go and what may be held on to, do not be too greatly influenced by Christians you may know and what they do. Go instead by the clear teaching of the Bible and by the prompting of your conscience, and Christ will gradually lead you further along the right path. When he puts his finger on anything, give it up. It may be someone you spend time with or something you do, or some attitude of pride, jealousy or resentment, or a refusal to forgive.

Jesus told his followers to gouge out their eye and cut off their hand or foot if these caused them to sin. We are not to obey this literally, of course, by mutilating our bodies. It is a vivid figure of speech for dealing ruthlessly with the ways through which temptation comes to us.

Sometimes, true repentance has to include making amends. This means putting things right with other people whom we may have hurt. All our sins wound God, and nothing we do can heal the injury. Only the atoning death of our Saviour, Jesus Christ, can do this. But when our sins have harmed other people, we can sometimes help to repair the damage, and where we can, we must. Zacchaeus, the dishonest tax-collector, more than repaid the money he had stolen from his clients and promised to give away half his capital to the poor to compensate for the thefts which he was unable to make good. We must follow his example. There may be money or time for us to pay back, rumours to be contradicted, property to return, apologies to be made, or broken relationships to be restored.

We must not be unduly overscrupulous in this matter, however. It would be foolish to rummage through past years and make an issue of insignificant words or deeds long ago forgotten by the person we offended. Nevertheless, we must be realistic about this duty. I have known a student own up to the university authorities that she had cheated in an exam, and another return some books which he had stolen from a shop. An army officer sent a list of items he had 'scrounged' to the Ministry of Defence. If we really repent, then we shall want to do everything in our power to put things right. We cannot continue to enjoy what we have gained from the sins we want to be forgiven.

Second, there must be *a renunciation of self.* In order to follow Christ, we must not only forsake isolated sins, but give up the very principle of self-will which lies at the root of every act of sin. To follow Christ is to surrender to him the rights over our own lives. It is to abdicate the throne of our heart and obey him as our King. This renunciation of self is vividly described by Jesus in three phrases.

It is to *deny ourselves*: 'Whoever wants to be my disciple must deny themselves.' The same verb is used of Peter's denial of his Lord in the courtyard of the high priest's palace after the arrest of Jesus. We are to disown ourselves as completely as Peter disowned Christ when he said, 'I don't know this man you're talking about.' Self-denial is not about just giving up occasional luxuries, either temporarily or even for good. It isn't a matter of denying *things* to myself, but of denying *myself* to myself. It is to say 'no' to self, and 'yes' to Christ; to demote self and give first place to Christ.

The next phrase Jesus used is to *take up the cross*: 'Whoever wants to be my disciple must deny themselves and take up their cross and follow me.' If we had lived in first-century Palestine and seen a man carrying his cross, we should at once have recognized him as a convicted prisoner being led out to be put to death. For Palestine was an occupied country, and this is what the Romans forced convicted criminals to do. In his commentary on Mark's Gospel, Professor H. B. Swete wrote that to take up the cross is 'to put oneself into the position of a condemned man on his way to execution'. In other words, the attitude to self which we are to adopt is that of crucifixion. Paul uses the same image when he declares that 'those who belong to Christ Jesus have crucified the sinful nature with its passions and desires'.

In Luke's version of this saying of Christ, the word 'daily' is added. Every day the Christian is to die. Every day we are to hand over the independence of our own will. Every day we are invited to renew our unconditional surrender to Jesus Christ.

The third expression which Jesus used to describe the renunciation of self is to *lose our life*: 'Whoever loses their life … will save it.' By 'life' here Jesus doesn't mean our physical existence or our soul, but our self. The *psyche* is the ego, the human personality which thinks, feels, plans and chooses. There's an important sense in which those who commit themselves to Christ lose themselves. But this does not mean that we lose our individuality. Our will is indeed submitted to Christ's will, but our personality is not absorbed into Christ's personality. On the contrary, as we shall see later, when we lose ourselves, we actually find ourselves and discover our true identity.

He does not call us to a sloppy half-heartedness, but to a vigorous, absolute commitment.

So, in order to follow Christ we have to deny ourselves, to crucify ourselves, to lose ourselves. The full, inescapable demand of Jesus Christ is now revealed in full. He does not call us to a sloppy half-heartedness, but to a vigorous, absolute commitment. He calls us to make him our Lord.

Many people think that we can enjoy the benefits of Christ's salvation without accepting the challenge of his absolute authority. There is no support for such an unbalanced idea in the New Testament. 'Jesus is Lord' is the earliest known summary of what Christians believe. At a time when the Roman Empire was pressing its citizens to say 'Caesar is Lord', these were dangerous words. But Christians did not flinch. They simply could not give Caesar their first allegiance. Why? Because they had already given it to the Emperor Jesus. God had placed his Son Jesus far above every other authority and given the highest possible status to him, so that 'every knee should bow' before him 'and every tongue confess that Jesus Christ is Lord'.[3]

To make Christ Lord is to bring every area of our public and private lives under his control. This includes our career. God has a purpose for every life. Our task is to discover it and fulfil it. God's plan may be different from our own ideas or those of our parents and friends. If we are wise, we will do nothing rash or reckless. We may already be occupied in, or preparing for, the work God has for us to do. But we may not. If Christ is our Lord, we must open our minds to the possibility of a change.

What is certain is that God calls every Christian to 'ministry', that is, to service, to be the servant of other people for the sake of Christ. We are no longer to live just for ourselves. What is not certain is what form this service will take. It might be the ordained ministry of the church, or some other kind of full-time church work in our own country or overseas. But it is a great mistake to suppose that every committed Christian is called to this. The truth is that every form of work in which we see ourselves as cooperating with God in the service of others merits the job description 'Christian ministry'.

Do not be in too great a hurry to discover God's will for your life. If you are prepared to do it and listening out for God to reveal what it is, he will let you know in his own time. Whatever it turns out to be, we are not to be idle as Christians. For whether we are an employer, an employee or self-employed, we have a heavenly Master. The challenge is for us to understand God's purpose in our work, and be whole-hearted about it, as if we were 'serving the Lord not people'.

Another area of life which belongs under the lordship of Jesus Christ is our marriage and our home. Jesus once said, 'Do not suppose that I have come to bring peace to the earth. I did not come to bring peace, but a sword.' He went on to speak of the clash of loyalties which sometimes arises within a family when one of its members begins to follow him.

Such family conflicts still take place today. We should never actively look for them. We have a clear duty to love and honour our parents and other members of our family. Since we are called to be peacemakers, we will make as many concessions as we can without compromising our duty to God. Yet we should never forget what Christ said: 'Anyone who loves his father or mother . . . son or daughter more than me is not worthy of me.'[4]

Going on from this, a Christian is free to marry only a Christian. The Bible is definite here: 'Do not be yoked together with unbelievers.'[5] This command can bring great distress to somebody who is already engaged or nearly so, but it must be honestly faced. Marriage is not merely a convenient social custom. It is something given to us by God. And the married relationship is the deepest into which human beings can enter. God designed it to be an intimate union, not only physical, emotional, intellectual and social, but spiritual. For a Christian to marry someone with whom he or she cannot be spiritually one is not only to disobey God, but to miss out on the full extent of what he intends marriage to be. It also puts the couple's children at risk by introducing religious tension in their own home and making the distinctively Christian nurture they should be receiving from both their parents impossible.

Indeed, Christian conversion is so radical that our whole attitude to marriage, and to the relationship between the sexes, is likely to change. We begin to see sexuality – the fundamental distinction between man and woman, and the need of the one for the other – as itself the creation of God. And sex – the physical expression of sexuality – is no longer spoiled by selfish irresponsibility and made into something casual and essentially impersonal. Instead it becomes what the Creator meant it to be, entirely good and right, the expression of love, bringing God's purpose to completion and fulfilling the human personality.

Other previously private matters over which Jesus Christ becomes Master, when we commit our lives to him, are our money and our time. Jesus often spoke about money, and about the danger of wealth. Much of his teaching on the subject is very disturbing. It sometimes seems as if he was recommending his disciples to sell everything they had and give it all away. No doubt he still calls some of his followers to do this today. But, for most of us, his command is to an inner detachment from money rather than to a literal rejection of what we have. The New Testament does not imply that possessions are sinful in themselves.

Christ certainly meant us to put him above material wealth just as we are to put him above family ties. We cannot serve God and money. It follows from this that we are also to be careful in the way that we use our money. We should think of it as no longer ours but as a resource we hold on trust from God.

And in a world in which the gap between rich and poor is getting wider all the time, and in which the work of Christian mission is often severely held back by lack of funds, we should be generous and disciplined in what we give away.

There are many things that compete for our time, and becoming a Christian will bring with it the need to reorganize our priorities. If we are students, academic work will come high on the list. Christians should be known for their hard work and honesty. But we will also need to make time for new things. It's important to take our busy schedules and carve out time for daily prayer and Bible reading, for setting Sunday apart as a day of worship and rest, for developing friendships with other Christians, for reading Christian literature, taking in Christian teaching, and for some kind of service in the church and the community.

All this is what is involved in forsaking sin and self, and following Christ.

THE CALL TO ACKNOWLEDGE CHRIST

We are commanded not only to follow Christ privately, but also to acknowledge him publicly. It is not enough to deny ourselves in secret if we deny him in the open. He said:

> If any of you are ashamed of me and my words in this adulterous and sinful generation, the Son of Man will be ashamed of you when he comes in his Father's glory with the holy angels.

> Whoever publicly acknowledges me I will also acknowledge before my Father in heaven. But whoever publicly disowns me I will disown before my Father in heaven.[6]

The very fact that Jesus told us not to be ashamed of him shows that he knew we would be tempted to be ashamed; and the fact that he added 'in this adulterous and sinful generation' shows that he knew why. He clearly anticipated that his church would be a minority movement in the world; and it requires courage to side with the few against the many, especially if the few are unpopular and we may not be naturally drawn to them.

Yet this open acknowledgment of Christ cannot be avoided. Paul declared it to be a condition of salvation. In order to be saved, he wrote, we need not only to believe in our hearts, but to confess with our lips that Jesus is Lord, 'for it is with your heart that you believe and are justified, and it is with your mouth that you confess and are saved'. He may have been referring to baptism, which is certainly something for new Christians to undergo (if they have not already been baptized). Baptism is partly about receiving through water the visible sign and seal of our inner cleansing and new life in Christ. But it is also about acknowledging publicly that we have trusted in Jesus Christ as our Saviour and Lord and now belong to him.

But acknowledging Christ is not limited to baptism. We must also be willing for our family and friends to know that we are Christians, especially at first by the way we live our lives. This is likely in due course to lead to opportunities to speak about our faith, although we need to be humble and honest here and not blunder tactlessly into other people's privacy. We also need to become members of a church and to join with other Christians at our school, college or place of work. We must not be afraid to own up to our Christian commitment when challenged about it. And we need to make it our aim to win our friends for Christ by praying for them, living in a way which honours God and taking opportunities to share our faith in conversation.

INCENTIVES

Jesus makes heavy demands; but he also gives compelling reasons for them. Indeed, if we are to be serious about the total surrender he asks for, we shall need these powerful incentives.

The first incentive is *for our own sake.*

> Whoever wants to save their life will lose it, but whoever loses their life for me and for the gospel will save it. What good is it for you to gain the whole world, yet forfeit your soul? Or what can you give in exchange for your soul?[7]

Many people have a deep-seated fear that, if they commit themselves to Jesus Christ, they will be the losers. They forget that Jesus came into the world that we might 'have life, and have it to the full', that his purpose is to make us rich not poor, and that to serve him is perfect freedom.

Of course there are losses to face when we submit to Christ. We have already thought about the sin and self-centredness which we have to put behind us; and we may lose some of our friends. But the rich and satisfying rewards more than compensate for any loss. The astonishing paradox of Christ's teaching and of Christian experience is that when we lose ourselves in following Christ, we actually find ourselves. True self-denial is true self-discovery. To live for ourselves is insanity and suicide; to live for God and for others is wisdom and life indeed. We do not begin to find ourselves until we have become willing to lose ourselves in the service of Christ and of others.

To reinforce this truth, Jesus drew a contrast between the whole world and the individual soul. He then asked a commercial question of profit and loss. Suppose you were to gain the whole world and lose yourself, he asked, what profit would you have made? He was arguing at the lowest level of personal advantage and pointing out that to follow him is undoubtedly to have the best deal. For to follow him is to find ourselves, whereas to hold on to ourselves and refuse to follow him is to lose ourselves and squander our eternal destiny, whatever material benefits we may have gained in the meantime. Why is this? Well, for one thing we cannot gain the whole world. Secondly, even if we did, it would not last. And, thirdly, while it did last, it would not satisfy. 'What can you give in exchange for your soul?' Nothing is valuable enough even to make an offer. Of course it costs to be a Christian; but it costs more not to be one.

The second incentive for Christian commitment is *for the sake of others*. We should not submit to Christ simply for what we get, but for what we can give. 'Whoever loses their life for . . . the gospel will save it.' 'For the gospel' means 'for the sake of making it known to others'. We have already seen that we must not be ashamed of Christ or of his words; now we are to be so proud of him that we want to spread his good news to others.

Most of us feel demoralized by the heart-rending tragedy of this chaotic world. Our very survival is in doubt. The ordinary citizen often feels a helpless victim of the tangled web of politics, or a faceless unit in the machine of modern society. But the Christian need not succumb to this sense of power-lessness. For Jesus Christ described his followers as both 'the salt of the earth' and 'the light of the world'. The use of salt before the invention of refrigeration was largely negative – to prevent decay in fish or meat. So Christians should stop society from deteriorating, by helping to preserve moral standards, influence public opinion and secure just legislation. As the light of the world, Christians are to let their light shine. They have found in Jesus Christ the secret of peace and love, of personal relationships, of changing people for the better; they must share their secret with others. The best contribution anyone can make to putting the world to rights is to live a Christian life, build a Christian home, and radiate the light of the gospel of Jesus Christ.

The greatest incentive of all, however, is *for Christ's sake*. 'Whoever loses their life for me ... will save it.' When we are asked to do something particularly hard, our willingness to do so depends very much on who asks us. If the request comes from someone to whom we owe a favour, we are glad to agree. This is what makes Christ's appeal to us so eloquent and so persuasive. He asks us to deny ourselves and follow him for his own sake.

This is why he describes the renunciation he demands as 'taking up the cross'. He asks no more than he himself gave. He asks a cross for a cross. So we should follow him not just for what we can get or for what we can give, but supremely because of what he gave. He gave himself. Will it cost us a great deal? It cost him more. He left the Father's glory, the security of heaven and the worship of countless angels when he came. He humbled himself to assume human nature, to be born in a stable and laid in a manger, to work at a carpenter's bench, to make friends with ordinary fishermen, to die on a criminal's cross, and to bear the sins of the world.

It is only as we see the cross that we become willing to deny ourselves and follow Christ. Our little crosses are far eclipsed by his. Once we catch a glimpse of the greatness of his love in willingly suffering such shame and pain for us who deserved nothing but judgment, only one course of action will be open to us. How can we deny or reject such a lover?

If, then, you suffer from moral anaemia, take my advice and steer clear of Christianity. If you want a life of easy-going self-indulgence, then do not, whatever you do, become a Christian. But if you want a life of self-discovery, deeply satisfying to the nature God has given you; if you want a life of adventure in which you have the privilege of serving him and other people; if you want a life in which to express something of the overwhelming gratitude you are beginning to feel for him who died for you, then I urge you to yield your life, without reservation and without delay, to your Lord and Saviour, Jesus Christ.

STUDY QUESTIONS

1. Why does it cost us something to follow Christ? What are you aware of that it would or does cost you?
2. 'Many people think that we can enjoy the benefits of Christ's salvation without accepting the challenge of his absolute authority.' What is wrong with this?
3. Are you in a position to know the shape of the 'ministry' to which God is calling you? How do you know?
4. What would or does it mean in practice for you to 'acknowledge Christ'?
5. What are the 'compelling reasons' that we are given for becoming fully committed to Christ?

Chapter 10

REACHING A
DECISION

The idea that a decision is needed in order to become a Christian strikes many people as very strange. Some imagine that they are already Christians because they were born in a Christian country. 'After all,' they say, 'we aren't Muslims, or Jews, or Hindus, or Buddhists; so we must be Christians!' Others think that if they have been brought up in a Christian home and taught to accept the Christian creed and Christian standards of behaviour, nothing further is required of them. But, whatever our background and upbringing, each of us as responsible adults must make up our own minds for or against Christ. We cannot remain neutral. Nor can we just drift into Christianity. Nor can anyone else settle the matter for us. We must decide for ourselves.

Even to agree with all that has so far been written in this book is not enough. We may admit that the evidence for the deity of Jesus is compelling, even conclusive, and that he was in fact the Son of God; we may believe that he came and died to be the Saviour of the world; we may also admit that we are sinners and need such a Saviour. But it isn't these things that make us Christians. To believe certain facts about who Christ is and what he has done for us is a vital first stage, but true faith must turn such mental belief into a decisive act of trust. Intellectual conviction must lead to personal commitment.

I myself used to think that, because Jesus had died on the cross, everyone in the world had been put right with God by some kind of rather mechanical transaction. I remember how puzzled, even offended, I was when it was first suggested to me that I needed to take hold of Christ and his salvation for myself. I thank God that he later opened my eyes to see that I must do more than face up to the fact that I needed *a* Saviour, more even than admit that Jesus Christ was *the* Saviour I needed; it was necessary to accept him as *my* Saviour. This way of putting things is certainly prominent in the Bible:

The LORD is *my* shepherd, I lack nothing.

The LORD is *my* light and *my* salvation.

O God, you are *my* God.

The surpassing greatness of knowing Christ Jesus *my* Lord.

One verse in the Bible, which has helped many seekers (including myself) to understand the step of faith we have to take, focuses on the words of Christ himself. He says: 'Here I am! I stand at the door and knock. If anyone hears my voice and opens the door, I will come in and eat with them, and they with me.'[1]

This verse was illustrated by Holman Hunt in his well-known picture 'The Light of the World', painted in 1853. The original hangs in the chapel of Keble College, Oxford, and a replica (painted by the artist himself forty years later) is in St Paul's Cathedral, London. The symbolism in the picture is very helpful. John Ruskin, in a letter to *The Times* back in May 1854, described it like this:

> ... On the left-hand side of the picture is seen this door of the human soul. It is fast barred; its bars and nails are rusty; it is knitted and bound to its stanchions by creeping tendrils of ivy, showing that it has never been opened. A bat hovers about it; its threshold is overgrown with brambles, nettles and fruitless corn ... Christ approaches it in the night-time ...

He is wearing a royal robe and a crown of thorns, holding a lantern in his left hand (as the light of the world) and knocking on the door with his right.

It's helpful to look at the context of this verse. It comes at the end of a letter addressed by Christ through John to the church of Laodicea, situated in what is now Turkey. Laodicea was a prosperous city, renowned for its manufacture of clothing, its medical school where the famous Phrygian eye powder was made, and its wealthy banks.

Material prosperity had brought with it a spirit of complacency which had even contaminated the Christian church. Attached to it were those who said they were committed to Christ, but were Christian in name only. They were tolerably respectable, but nothing more. Their religious interest was shallow and casual. Like the water from the hot springs of Hierapolis, which was piped to Laodicea by conduits (the remains of which can still be seen), they were (Jesus said) neither hot nor cold, but lukewarm, and therefore nauseating to him. Their spiritual half-heartedness is explained in terms of self-delusion: 'You say, "I am rich; I have acquired wealth and do not need a thing." But you do not realize that you are wretched, pitiful, poor, blind and naked.'

What a description of proud and prosperous Laodicea! They were blind and naked beggars – naked despite their clothing factory, blind despite their eye ointment, and beggars despite their banks.

We are no different today. Perhaps we say, as they did, 'I don't need anything.' It's hard to think of words more spiritually dangerous. It is our self-contained independence which, more than anything else, keeps us from committing ourselves to Christ. Of course we need him! Without him we are morally naked (with no clothing to make us fit for God's presence), blind to spiritual truth, and beggars, having nothing with which to buy the treasure of heaven. But Christ can clothe us with his righteousness, touch our eyes so that we can see and enrich us with spiritual wealth. Apart from him, and until we open the door to let him in, we are blind and naked beggars.

'Here I am! I stand at the door and knock,' he says. He is no figment of the imagination, no fictional character from a religious novel. This is the man of Nazareth, whose claims, character and resurrection support the conclusion that he is the Son of God. He is also the crucified Saviour. The hand that knocks is scarred. The feet which stand on the doorstep still bear the print of nails.

And he is the risen Christ. John has already described him in the first chapter of Revelation, as he saw him in a vision full of symbol. His eyes were like blazing fire and his feet like bronze glowing in a furnace. His voice thundered like the breakers on the rocks and his face was radiant like the sun shining in all its brilliance. No wonder John fell at his feet. It is hard to understand how a person of such majesty could ever stoop to visit poor, blind and naked beggars like us.

Yet Jesus Christ says he is standing knocking at the door of our lives, waiting. Notice that he is standing at the door, not pushing it; speaking to us, not shouting. This is all the more remarkable when we reflect that the house is his in any case. He is the architect; he designed it. He is the builder; he made it. He is the landlord; he bought it with his own blood. So it is his by right of plan, construction and purchase. We are only tenants in a house which does not belong to us. He could put his shoulder to the door; he prefers to put his hand to the knocker. He could command us to open to him; instead, he merely invites us to do so. He will not force an entry into anybody's life. He says (v. 18), 'I counsel you . . .' He could issue orders; he is content to give advice. This is the nature of his humility and the extent of the freedom he has given us.

But why does Jesus Christ want to come in? We know the answer already. He wants to be both our Saviour and our Lord.

He died to be our Saviour. If we receive him, he will be able to apply to us personally all the benefits of his death. Once inside the house, he will renovate, redecorate and refurnish it. That is, he will cleanse and forgive us; our past will be blotted out. He promises too to eat with us and allow us to eat with him. The phrase describes the joy of having him as a companion. He not only gives himself to us but asks us to give ourselves to him. We have been strangers; now we are friends. There has been a closed door between us; now we are seated at the same table.

Jesus Christ will also enter as our Lord and Master. The house of our lives will come under his management, and there is no point in opening the door unless we are willing for this to happen. As he steps across the threshold, we must hand him our whole bunch of keys, granting him free access into every room. A fourth-year Canadian student once wrote to me,

'Instead of giving Christ a whole set of different keys to the many rooms of the house . . . I have given him a pass key to the whole lot.'

This involves repentance, turning decisively from everything we know that displeases him. Not that we make ourselves better before we invite him in. On the contrary, it is precisely because we cannot forgive or improve ourselves that we need him to come to us. But we must be willing for him to do whatever rearranging he likes when he has come in. There can be no resistance, and no attempt to negotiate our own terms, but rather an unconditional surrender to the lordship of Christ. What will this mean? I cannot tell you the details. But in principle it means a determination to forsake evil and follow Christ.

Do you hesitate? Do you feel that it is unreasonable to submit to Christ in the dark? It really isn't. It is much more reasonable than marriage, for example. In marriage a man and a woman commit themselves to each other unconditionally. They do not know what the future holds for them. But they love each other, and they trust each other. So they promise to take each other, 'to have and to hold from this day forward, for better for worse, for richer for poorer, in sickness and in health, to love and to cherish, till death us do part'. If human beings can trust one another like this, surely we can trust God's Son! It is more reasonable to commit oneself to him than to the finest human being. He will never betray us or let us down.

So what must we do? To begin with, we must hear his voice. It is tragically possible to turn a deaf ear to Christ and drown out the insistent whisper of his call. Sometimes we hear his voice through our conscience, sometimes as our minds reach out for the truth. Or it may be a sense of guilt, or the seeming emptiness and meaninglessness of our existence, or a mystifying spiritual hunger, or sickness, bereavement, pain or fear, by which we become aware that Christ is outside the door and speaking to us. Or his call can come to us through a friend, a preacher or a book. Whenever we hear, we must listen. 'Whoever has ears to hear,' Jesus says, 'let them hear.'

Next, we must open the door. Having heard his voice, we must open to his knock. To open the door to Jesus Christ is a graphic way of describing an act of faith in him as our Saviour, an act of submission to him as our Lord.

It is a definite act. The tense of the Greek verb makes this plain. The door does not happen to swing open by chance. Nor is it already slightly ajar. It is closed, and needs to be opened. Moreover, Christ will not open the door himself. There is no handle or latch on the door in Holman Hunt's picture. It is said that he deliberately left them out, to show that the handle was on the inside. Christ knocks; but we must open.

Each of us must make our own decision and take this step ourselves ... your hand and only yours can draw back the bolts and turn the handle.

It is an individual act. It's true that the message in Revelation was sent to a church, the nominal, lukewarm church of Laodicea. But the challenge is addressed to individuals within it: 'If *anyone* hears my voice and opens the door, I will come in and eat with them.' Each of us must make our own decision and take this step ourselves. No-one else can do it for you. Christian parents and teachers, ministers and friends can point the way, but your hand and only yours can draw back the bolts and turn the handle.

It is a unique act. You can take this step only once. When Christ has entered, he will bolt and bar the door on the inside. Sin may drive him into the cellar or the attic, but he will never altogether abandon the house he has entered. 'Never will I leave you; never will I forsake you,' he says. This is not to say that you emerge from this experience with the fully-grown wings of an angel! Nor that you will become perfect just like that. You can become a Christian in a moment, but not a mature Christian. Christ can enter, cleanse and forgive you in a matter of seconds, but it will take much longer for your character to be transformed and shaped to his will. It takes only a few minutes for a bride and bridegroom to be married, but it may take many years for two strong wills to become truly united as one. It is the same when we receive Christ: a moment of commitment will lead to a lifetime of adjustment.

It is a deliberate act. You do not have to wait for a supernatural light to flash upon you from heaven, or for an emotional experience to overwhelm you. No. Christ came into the world and died for your sins. He now stands outside the front door of the house of your life, and he is knocking. The next move is yours. His hand is already on the knocker; your hand must now feel for the latch.

It is an urgent act. Do not wait longer than you must. Time is passing. The future is uncertain. You may never have a better opportunity than this. 'Do not boast about tomorrow, for you do not know what a day may bring.' 'The Holy Spirit says, "Today, if you hear his voice, do not harden your hearts..." '2 Do not put it off until you have succeeded in making yourself a better person and more worthy to receive Christ; or until you have solved all your problems. It is enough simply to believe that Jesus Christ is the Son of God and that he died to be your Saviour. The rest will follow in time. It's true that there is danger in rushing into things too hastily; but there is equal danger in holding back unnecessarily. If you know in your heart of hearts that you should act, then you should not delay any longer.

It is an indispensable act. Of course there is much more to the Christian life than this. As we shall see in the next chapter, there is getting involved in the life of the church, discovering and doing God's will, growing in grace and understanding, and seeking to serve God and others; but this step is the beginning, and nothing else will do instead. You can believe in Christ intellectually and admire him; you can say your prayers to him through the keyhole (I did for many years); you can push coins at him under the door to keep him quiet; you can be moral, decent, upright and good; you can be religious; you can have been baptized and confirmed; you can be deeply versed in the philosophy of religion; you can be a theological student and even an ordained minister – and still not have opened the door to Christ. There is no substitute for this.

In his autobiography *Surprised by Joy*, Professor C. S. Lewis describes how he was travelling one day on the top of a bus, when

> without words and (I think) almost without images, a fact about myself was somehow presented to me. I became aware that I was holding something at bay, or shutting something out. Or, if you like, that I was wearing some stiff clothing, like corsets, or even a suit of armour, as if I were a lobster. I felt myself being, there and then, given a free choice. I could open the door or keep it shut; I could unbuckle the armour or keep it on. Neither choice was presented as a duty; no threat or promise was attached to either, though I knew that to open the door or to take off the corset meant the incalculable ... I chose to open, to unbuckle, to loosen the rein. I say 'I chose', yet it did not really seem possible to do the opposite.

A lady responded to Billy Graham's invitation to go forward at the end of an evangelistic meeting. She was introduced to an adviser who discovered that she had not yet committed her life to Christ and suggested that she should pray there and then. Bowing her head, she said, 'Dear Lord Jesus, I want you to come into my heart more than anything else in the world. Amen.'

A teenager knelt down by his bed one Sunday night in the dormitory of his school. In a simple, matter-of-fact but definite way, he told Christ that he had made rather a mess of life so far; he confessed his sins; he thanked Christ for dying for him; and he asked him to come into his life. The following day he wrote in his diary:

> Yesterday really *was* an eventful day! ... Up till now Christ has been on the circumference and I have but asked him to guide me instead of giving him complete control. Behold, he stands at the door and knocks. I have heard him and now he has come into my house. He has cleansed it and now rules in it...

And the day after:

> I really have felt an immense and new joy throughout today. It is the joy of being at peace with the world and of being in touch with God. How well do I know now that he rules me and that I never really knew him before...

These are extracts from my own diary. I quote them because I do not want you to think that I am recommending to you a step which I have not taken myself.

Are you a Christian? A real and committed Christian? Your answer depends on another question – not whether you go to church or not, believe the creed or not, or lead a decent life or not (important as all these are in their place), but rather this: which side of the door is Jesus Christ? Is he inside or outside? That is the crucial issue.

Perhaps you are ready to open the door to Christ. If you are not sure whether you have ever done so, my advice to you would be to make sure, even if (as someone has put it) you will be going over in ink what you have already written in pencil.

I suggest that you get away by yourself to pray. Admit your sins to God, and resolve to have done with them. Thank Jesus Christ that he died for your sake and in your place. Then open the door and ask him to come in as your personal Saviour and Lord.

You might find it a help to echo this prayer in your heart:

Lord Jesus Christ, I acknowledge that I have gone my own way. I have sinned in thought, word and deed. I am sorry for my sins. I turn from them in repentance.

I believe that you died for me, bearing my sins in your body on the cross. I thank you for your great love.

Now I open the door. Come in, Lord Jesus. Come in as my Saviour, and cleanse me. Come in as my Lord, and take control of me. And I will serve as you give me strength, all my life. Amen.

If you have prayed this prayer and meant it, humbly thank Christ that he has come in. For he said he would. He has given his word: 'If anyone hears my voice and opens the door, *I will come in* and eat with them . . .' Don't worry about how you may or may not be feeling, but trust his promise and thank him that he has kept his word.

STUDY QUESTIONS

1. Why is becoming a Christian something we 'must decide for ourselves'? How does Holman Hunt's picture 'The Light of the World' depict this?
2. Why doesn't Christ 'force an entry into anybody's life'?
3. How would you help someone who feels that it is 'unreasonable to submit to Christ in the dark'? How does the illustration of marriage help here?
4. In practical terms, what difference does 'a determination to forsake evil and follow Christ' mean for you?

Chapter 11

BEING
A CHRISTIAN

This last chapter is written for those who have opened the door of their lives to Jesus Christ. They have committed themselves to him. They have thus begun the Christian life. But *becoming* a Christian is one thing; *being* a Christian is another. So we turn now to what it means to live as a Christian.

You took a simple step; you invited Christ to come as your Saviour and Lord. At that moment what can only be described as a miracle took place. God – without whose grace you could not have repented and believed – gave you a new life. You were born again. You became a child of God and so entered his family. You may not have been conscious of anything happening, just as at the time of your physical birth you were not aware of what was taking place. Self-consciousness, the awareness of who and what one is, is part of the process of personal development. Nevertheless, just as when you were born you emerged as a new independent personality, so when you were born again you became spiritually a new creature in Christ.

But (you may be thinking) is not God the Father of
everyone? Are not all people the children of God? Yes and no!
God is certainly the Creator of all, and we are all his 'offspring'
in the sense that we all derive our being from him.[1] But the
Bible clearly distinguishes between this general relationship
which God has with the whole human race as Creator and the
special relationship as Father which he establishes with those
who are his new creation through Jesus Christ. John explains
this in the introduction to his Gospel when he writes:

> He [that is, Jesus] came to that which was his own, but his own did
> not receive him. Yet to all who received him, to those who believed
> in his name, he gave the right to become children of God ... born
> of God.

Different ways of describing the same people are being used
here. The children of God are those who are born of God; and
those who are born of God are those who have received Christ
into their lives and who have believed in his name.

What does it mean to be a 'child' of God in this sense? Like
membership of any other family, it has both its privileges and
its responsibilities. We go on now to see what these are.

CHRISTIAN PRIVILEGES

The unique privilege of those who have been born into the
family of God is that they have a new relationship with God.

An intimate relationship

We saw earlier that our sins alienated us from God. They came
as a barrier between us. To put it another way, we were under
the just condemnation of the Judge of all the earth. But now
through Jesus Christ, who bore that condemnation for us and

with whom we have become united by faith, we have been 'justified', that is, accepted by God and declared to be righteous. Our Judge has become our Father.

'See what great love the Father has lavished on us, that we should be called children of God! And that is what we are!' wrote John. 'Father' and 'Son' are the distinctive titles which Jesus used of God and himself, and they are the very names which he encourages us to use too! Through our relationship with him we are allowed to share something of his own close relationship with the Father. Cyprian, Bishop of Carthage in the middle of the third century AD, gives a brilliant description of the privilege this is in what he writes about the Lord's Prayer:

> How great is the Lord's indulgence! How great are his condescension and plenteousness of goodness towards us, seeing that he has wished us to pray in the sight of God in such a way as to call God Father, and to call ourselves sons of God, even as Christ is the Son of God – a name which none of us would dare to venture on in prayer, unless he himself had allowed us thus to pray.

Now at last we can say the Lord's Prayer without hypocrisy. Previously the words had a rather hollow sound; now they ring with new and wonderful meaning. God is indeed our Father in heaven, who knows our needs before we ask and will not fail to give good things to his children.

It may sometimes be necessary for us to be corrected by him, 'because the Lord disciplines those he loves, and he chastens everyone he accepts as his child'. But in this he is simply treating us as members of his family and disciplining us for our good. With such a loving, wise and strong Father, we can be delivered from all our fears.[2]

An assured relationship

The Christian's relationship to God as a child to his or her Father is not only intimate, but sure. So many people seem to do no more than hope for the best when it is possible to know for certain.

In fact it is more than possible. It is what God has said he wants for us. We should be sure of our relationship with God not just for our peace of mind and the ability to help others, but because God means us to be sure. John clearly states that this was why he wrote his first letter: 'I write this to you who believe in the name of the Son of God, that you may know that you have eternal life.'

Yet the way to *be* sure is not just to *feel* sure. Many people who are at the beginning of their Christian life make this mistake. They rely too much on their superficial feelings. One day they *feel* close to God; the next day they *feel* alienated from him again. And since they think that their feelings are an accurate reflection of their spiritual condition, they fall into a frenzy of uncertainty. Their Christian life becomes a precarious roller coaster as they soar to the heights of ecstasy, only to plunge again into the depths of depression.

Such an up-and-down experience is not what God intends for his children. We have to learn to be wary of our feelings. They are extremely variable. They change with the weather, with circumstances and with our health. We are unpredictable creatures of whim and mood, and our fluctuating feelings often have nothing to do with our spiritual progress.

The basis of how we know that we are in relationship with God is not how we feel, but the fact that he says we are. The test we are to apply to ourselves is objective rather than subjective. We are not to ferret around inside ourselves for evidence of spiritual life, but to look up and out and away to God and his word. But where shall we find God's word to assure us that we are his children?

First, God promises in his written word to give eternal life to those who receive Christ. 'This is the testimony: God has given us eternal life, and this life is in his Son. Whoever has the Son has life; whoever does not have the Son of God does not have life.' To believe in all humility that we have eternal life is not presumptuous. On the contrary, to trust what God says is humility not pride, and wisdom rather than presumption. The foolishness and the sin would be to entertain doubts, for 'whoever does not believe God has made him out to be a liar, because they have not believed the testimony God has given about his Son'.[3]

Now the Bible is full of God's promises. It's a good idea to begin as soon as possible to commit them to memory. Then when we fall into the ditch of depression and doubt, we can use God's promises as ropes with which to pull ourselves out.

Here are a few verses to start memorizing. Each contains a divine promise.[4]

- Christ will receive us if we come to him: John 6:37.
- He will hold us and never let us go: John 10:28.
- He will never leave us: Matthew 28:20; Hebrews 13:5–6.
- God will not allow us to be tempted beyond our strength: 1 Corinthians 10:13.
- He will forgive us when we confess our sins: 1 John 1:9.
- He will give us wisdom when we ask for it: James 1:5.

Secondly, God speaks to our hearts. Look at these statements. 'God has poured out his love into our hearts by the Holy Spirit...' and 'You received the Spirit of sonship. And by him we cry, "*Abba*, Father." The Spirit himself testifies with our spirit that we are God's children.'[5] Every Christian knows what this means. The outward witness of the Holy Spirit in the Bible is confirmed by the inward witness of the Holy Spirit in our experience. This is not to place any confidence in superficial and changeable feelings; it is rather about expecting a deepening conviction in our hearts as the Holy Spirit assures us of God's love for us and prompts us to call out 'Father!' as we seek God's face in prayer.

Thirdly, the same Spirit who underlines the reality of our relationship with the Father in Scripture and experience completes this work in our character. If we are born again into God's family, then God's Spirit lives within us. Indeed, this indwelling of the Holy Spirit is one of the greatest privileges of God's children. It is the characteristic that marks us out: 'For those who are led by the Spirit of God are the children of God.' Again, 'If anyone does not have the Spirit of Christ, they do not belong to Christ.'[6] And he will not have lived in us very long before he begins to make changes to the way we live. In his first letter John applies this test ruthlessly. If anyone persists in disobeying God's commands and in disregarding his duties to other people, he writes, then he is not a Christian, whatever he may say. Righteousness and love are indispensable marks of the child of God.

A secure relationship

Let us suppose that we have entered into this intimate relationship with God, and are confident of it on the basis of God's word. How secure a relationship is it? Can we be born into God's family one moment and turfed out of it the next? The Bible indicates that it is a permanent relationship. 'If children, then heirs,' wrote Paul, 'heirs of God and co-heirs with Christ', and went on to argue, in a magnificent passage at the end of

Romans 8, that God's children are eternally safe, for there is absolutely nothing which can separate them from his love.

'But what happens if and when I sin?' you may ask. 'Do I then lose my status in God's family and cease to be his child?' No. Think of the analogy of a human family. Imagine a boy being offensively rude to his parents. A cloud descends on the home. There is tension in the atmosphere. Father and son are not on speaking terms. What has happened? Has the boy ceased to be a son? No. Their relationship is just the same; it is their fellowship which has been broken. Relationship depends on birth; fellowship depends on behaviour. As soon as the boy apologizes, he is forgiven. And forgiveness restores fellowship. Meanwhile, his relationship has remained the same. He may temporarily have been a disobedient, and even a defiant, son; but at no point did he stop being a son.

It is just the same with the children of God. When we sin, we do not lose our relationship to him as children, though our fellowship with him is spoiled until we confess and turn away from our sin. As soon as we 'confess our sins, he is faithful and just and will forgive us our sins and purify us from all unrighteousness', for 'if anybody does sin, we have an advocate with the Father – Jesus Christ, the Righteous One. He is the atoning sacrifice for our sins'.[7] So do not wait until the evening, let alone the following Sunday, to put right whatever has gone wrong during each day. Instead, as soon as you are conscious of having fallen into sin, repent straight away and humbly seek your Father's forgiveness. Aim to keep your conscience clean and clear.

To put it another way, we can be justified only once; but we need to be forgiven every day. Jesus gave his disciples an illustration of this when he washed their feet on the evening before his trial and crucifixion. Peter asked him to wash his hands and his head as well as his feet. But Jesus replied, 'Those who have had a bath need only to wash their feet; their whole body is clean.' A guest invited to a dinner party in Jerusalem would take a bath before setting out. On arrival at their friend's house, they would not be offered another bath; but a servant would meet them at the front door and wash their feet. When we first come to Christ in repentance and faith, we receive a 'bath' (which is justification, for which baptism is the outward symbol). It never needs to be repeated. But as we walk through the dusty streets of the world, we constantly need to 'have our feet washed' (which is daily forgiveness).

CHRISTIAN RESPONSIBILITIES

To be a child of God is a wonderful privilege, but it also involves obligations. Peter implied this when he wrote:

'Like newborn babies, crave pure spiritual milk, so that by it you may grow up in your salvation.'[8]

> *Our great privilege as children of God is relationship; our great responsibility is growth.*

Our great privilege as children of God is relationship; our great responsibility is growth. People love children, but nobody in their right mind wants them to stay in the nursery. The tragedy, however, is that many Christians, genuinely born again in Christ, never grow up. Others even suffer from spiritual infantile regression. Our heavenly Father's purpose, on the other hand, is that 'babies in Christ' should become 'mature in Christ'. Our birth must be followed by growth. The once-for-all crisis of justification (our acceptance before God) must lead to the continuing process of sanctification (our growth in holiness, what Peter means by 'growing up in our salvation').

There are two main areas in which we are meant to grow as Christians. The first is in understanding and the second in holiness. When we begin the Christian life, most of us understand very little, and we have only just come to know God. Now we must grow in the knowledge of God and of our Lord and Saviour, Jesus Christ. This knowledge is partly intellectual and partly personal. To help with the first, I would urge you not only to study the Bible, but also to read good Christian books. To neglect to grow in your understanding is to risk disaster.

We must also grow in holiness of life. The New Testament writers speak of the development of our faith in God, our love for others and our likeness to Christ. Every child of God longs to become more and more like Jesus in their character and behaviour. The Christian life is a life of righteousness. We are to make it our aim to obey God's commandments and do God's will. This is another of the reasons why the Holy Spirit has been given to us. He has made our bodies his temple. He dwells within us. And as we knuckle down under his authority and follow his leading, he will tame our evil desires and cause his fruit to appear in our lives, which is 'love, joy, peace, patience, kindness, goodness, faithfulness, gentleness and self-control'.[9]

But how shall we grow? There are three main secrets of spiritual development. They are also the main responsibilities of the child of God.

Our duty to God

Our relationship to our heavenly Father, though secure, is not static. He wants his children to grow up to know him more and more intimately. Generations of Christians have discovered that the best way to do this is to spend time with him every day in Bible reading and prayer. This is an essential for the Christian who wants to make progress. We are all busy nowadays, but we must somehow rearrange our priorities in order to make time for it. It will mean firm self-discipline, but granted this, together with an alarm clock that works, we are well on the road to victory.

It is important to maintain the balance between Bible reading and prayer, because God speaks to us through the Bible while we speak to him through prayer. It is also a good idea to be systematic in our reading of the Bible. Various methods are available.[10] Pray before you read, asking the Holy Spirit to open your eyes and bring light to your mind. Then read slowly, meditatively and thoughtfully. Read and reread the passage. Wrestle with it till its meaning becomes clear. Use a modern translation. The New International Version is probably the most accurate revision available in contemporary English. You may also find a good commentary a help.[11] Then go on to apply the message of the verses you have read to your own life. Look for promises to claim and commands to obey, examples to follow and sins to avoid. It is helpful to keep a notebook and write down what you learn. Above all, look for Jesus Christ. He is the chief subject of the Bible. We can not only find him revealed there, but can meet him personally through its pages.

Prayer follows naturally. Begin by speaking back to God on the same subject on which he has spoken to you. Don't change the conversation! If he has spoken to you of himself and his glory, worship him. If he has spoken to you of yourself and your sins, confess them. Thank him for any blessings which may have been revealed in the passage, and pray that its lessons may be learned by you and your friends.

When you have prayed over the Bible passage you have read, you will want to go on with other prayers. If your Bible is the first great aid to prayer, let your diary be the second. Commit to him the details of the day which lies before you in the morning, and run through the day again in the evening, confessing the sins you have committed, giving thanks for the blessings you have received and praying for the people you have met.

God is your Father. Be natural, confiding and bold. He is interested in all the details of your life. Very soon you will find that you need to begin to keep some kind of prayer list of your relatives and friends for whom you feel a responsibility to pray. Make your list as flexible as possible, so that people can be easily added to it or taken from it.

Our duty to the church

The Christian life is not just a private affair of your own. If we are born again into God's family, not only has he become our Father, but every other believer in the world, whatever their nation or denomination, has become our brother or sister in Christ. One of the commonest ways of describing Christians in the New Testament is as 'brothers and sisters'. This is a glorious truth. But it is no good imagining that membership of the universal church of Christ is enough; we must belong to some local branch of it. Nor is it sufficient to be a member of a Christian Union in a college or elsewhere (although I hope you will become active in yours if you are a student). Every Christian needs to belong to a local church and share in its worship, fellowship and witness.

You may ask which church you should join. If you are already linked with a church, either one you have been brought up in or one that you have been attending recently, it's sensible to stay where you are unless there's a good reason to leave and find somewhere else. But if you need to choose a church from scratch, here are two suggestions to guide you. The first concerns the minister, the second the congregation. Ask yourself these questions. Does the minister submit to the authority of the Bible, so that they aim in their sermons to explain its message and relate it to contemporary life? And does the congregation seem to be a genuine fellowship of believers who love Christ, one another and the world?

Baptism is the way of entry into the Christian community. It has other meanings as well, as we have seen, but if you have not been baptized, you should ask your minister to prepare you for baptism. Then do allow yourself to be drawn right into the Christian family. There is a lot that may seem strange to you at first, but do not hold back. Going to church on Sundays is a definite Christian duty, and nearly every branch of the Christian church agrees that the Lord's Supper or Holy Communion is the central act of worship, established by Christ as the way in which we remember his death in fellowship with one another.

I hope I am not giving the impression that relating to other Christians is just about joining together in worship! The challenge to demonstrate genuine love for our Christian brothers and sisters – rather than just spend time with them in church services – may seem rather daunting, but is a real and wonderful experience. A healthy Christian fellowship includes people of all types, backgrounds and ages, and there are new depths of friendship and mutual sharing to be discovered. Our closest friends will probably be Christians and, above all, our life partner must be one too.[12]

Our duty to the world around us
The Christian life is a family affair, in which the children enjoy fellowship with their Father and with each other. But we must

not for a moment imagine that this exhausts the Christian's responsibilities. We are not to be inward-looking and interested only in ourselves. On the contrary, every Christian should be deeply concerned about others. And it is part of our Christian calling to serve them in whatever ways we can.

The Christian church has a fine record of charitable work for the needy and neglected people of the world – the poor and hungry, the sick, the victims of oppression and discrimination, slaves, prisoners, orphans, refugees and life's casualties. And the work goes on. All over the world the followers of Christ are seeking in his name to alleviate suffering and distress. Yet there is an enormous amount still to be done. And sometimes, we have to admit with shame, others seem to show more compassion than we who claim to know Christ.

There is another and particular responsibility which Christians have towards 'the world', as the Bible describes those outside Christ and his church: evangelism. To 'evangelize' means literally to spread the good news of Jesus Christ. There are still millions of people who are ignorant of him and his salvation, in every part of the world. For centuries the church seems to have been half asleep. The challenge is for us to be Christians who are wide awake and active in seeking to win the world for Christ. It may be that he has a special task for you to do as an ordained minister of the gospel or as a missionary. If you are a student already launched on your course, it would be quite wrong for you to do anything rash or hasty. But seek to discover God's will for your life, and be ready to do it, whatever it is and wherever it may take you.

Although not every Christian is called to be a minister or a missionary, God does intend each of us as Christians to be a witness to Jesus Christ. In our own homes, among our friends and with our colleagues, we carry the solemn responsibility to live a consistent, loving, humble, honest, Christlike life, and to seek to win other people for him. We need to be discreet and courteous, but determined.

The way to begin is by prayer. Ask God to give you a special concern for one or two of your friends. Stick to people of your own sex and about your own age. Then pray regularly and definitely for their conversion; cultivate your friendship with them for its own sake; take trouble to spend time with them; and really love them for themselves. Soon an opportunity will come to take them to some event where they will hear the good news of Jesus explained; or to give them some Christian literature to read; or to tell them simply what Jesus Christ has come to mean to you and how you found him. I need hardly add that the most convincing testimony will be ineffective if we are contradicting it by the way we behave; while little is more influential for Christ than a life which he is obviously transforming.

These then are the great privileges and responsibilities of the child of God. Born into the family of God and enjoying a relationship with our heavenly Father which is intimate, assured and secure, we aim to be disciplined in our daily times of Bible reading and prayer, loyal in our church membership, and at the same time active in Christian service and witness.

This statement of the Christian life reveals the tension which is faced by all Christians. To put it in a nutshell, we find ourselves citizens of two kingdoms, possessing dual nationality, the one earthly and the other heavenly. And each citizenship brings duties which we are not free to avoid.

On the one hand, the New Testament writers lay considerable stress on our obligations to the state, to our employer, to our family and to society as a whole. The Bible will not allow us to retreat from these practical responsibilities into mystical seclusion or into a so-called Christian fellowship which tries to insulate itself from the world.

On the other hand, some New Testament authors remind us that we are 'aliens and strangers' on earth, that 'our citizenship is in heaven' and that we are travelling to an eternal home.[13] Consequently, we are not to store up treasures on earth, nor to pursue purely selfish ambitions, nor to become assimilated to the standards of the world around us, nor to be unduly weighed down by the sorrows of this present life.

It is comparatively simple to ease this tension either by withdrawing into Christ and neglecting the world, or by so involving ourselves in the world as to forget Christ. Neither of these is a genuinely Christian solution, however, since each leads us to deny one or other of our Christian obligations. The balanced Christian who takes the Bible as their guide will seek to live equally and simultaneously 'in Christ' and 'in the world'. We cannot opt out of either.

This is the life of discipleship to which Jesus Christ calls us. He died and rose again that we might live a new life. He has given us his Spirit so that we can live out this life in the world.

Now he calls us to follow him, to give ourselves completely and unreservedly to his service.

STUDY QUESTIONS

1. How does the statement that 'everyone is a child of God' need to be qualified? Why is this?
2. What are the consequences that follow from being able to describe God as our Father?
3. How can we be certain of our relationship with God? How would you help someone who said that they didn't feel sure about this?

4. What do you see as the responsibilities that come with seeking to live as a Christian? What resources does God give to help?

5. Why does every Christian need 'to belong to a local church'? What does this involve?

6. In what ways are Christians to serve those in the world around them?

Appendix

THE IMPACT OF
BASIC CHRISTIANITY

This morning a Japanese copy of *Basic Christianity* was returned to me by the mother of a Japanese missionary. She's now looking for an opportunity of publicly confessing Christ. Many, many times Japanese (usually students) ... have been helped to find the Lord through this book.
From an OMF missionary in Japan, 1993

... I recently received a call from the chaplain of a prison (north of Sydney, Australia). I have been supplying the chaplain with books ... and he was happy to tell me a Turkish young man had become a Christian and it was the book *Basic Christianity* in Turkish which had given him a clear understanding of Christianity and the truth.
Australia, 2001

Upon hearing my first sermon after twenty years of intellectual indifference, I knew that the time had come to find out whether the claims of Jesus Christ were actually true! A wise person suggested five small books: Matthew, Mark, Luke, John, and Stott. Only 140 pages long, *Basic Christianity* makes a thorough statement of the biblical position that Jesus is God...

From a church newsletter book review (1992); the letter writer says he first read the book in 1976

I have learned and studied some years your book *Basic Christianity*, and the blessings I got from it could not be measured. I hope and believe that all who read would get the blessings of God enormously and tremendously, I am sure.

From a mission secretary, Myanmar, 1990

I grew up in a Christian home ... although I tried many times to be a Christian I was never successful ... I turned to Spiritualism ... began to drink heavily ... suffered from depression and suicidal tendencies.

About a year ago ... God began to work in my life ... I began to read my Bible and promised God that if he answered my questions I would become a Christian. One day I found a copy of *Basic Christianity* on my bookshelf. It had been there for fifteen to twenty years. The book convinced me that God was real and that Jesus really did die on the cross for my sins. It also said that the answers to my questions would be revealed to me only after I had committed my life to Christ. I knelt down ... and committed my life to Christ. Words cannot describe the joy and peace that came over me...

From a correspondent in South Africa, 1990

Yesterday, I spoke at [a] seminary chapel in Manila. With me was Abdul ... who gave a great testimony. He is a Muslim-background Filipino...

While in college he was witnessed to by a Filipina Christian who gave him one of your books. I think it was *Basic Christianity*. He read it three times and it was used to bring him to Christ.
From a missionary in the Philippines, 1989

On February 17, 1986 I found our Lord. It was through your book *Basic Christianity* that I was able to open my eyes and more importantly my heart. What a precious gift I have found through your writings.
From a lady correspondent in the US, 1987

Just finished reading *Basic Christianity*, and your approach to God has touched me beyond words. I am reading the Bible with more understanding now thanks to you and the Spirit ... I am presently in prison for the second time ... and really tired of living a negative life. Please pray for me.
From a US prison, 1986

I should have written this letter years ago ... However, this is the appropriate time of my life to ... write and say a very deep 'thank you' for being a powerful instrument in God's hand.
    ... Although I was from a 'religious' background, I had never heard of a personal relationship with Jesus Christ ... Then one day, my mother-in-law gave me a book by you called *Basic Christianity*. I accepted the book only because I did not want to hurt the feelings of one of the most kind and loving persons I had ever known ... I put the book aside for several months with no intention to read it. However, I was short of reading material one flight, and I hurriedly grabbed this book as I was rushing to leave for Amsterdam ...

It was in a little room in Amsterdam that I read your book and fully committed my life to Jesus. I was flooded with unbelievable love and transformed in character...
From a former pilot, now an ordained minister, 1982

I am writing to you as the one-year anniversary of a very important time in my life approaches ... [A year ago] through the action of the Holy Spirit, with your book *Basic Christianity* as one of the instruments, I came to know Jesus Christ as my Saviour.

When I came to chapter 10, 'Making a decision', I was ready to change my life...
From a correspondent in Oklahoma, 1980

When translating your book I've got the feeling that I know you personally. Your book has strengthened my belief and explained much that was unclear to me before.
From a Swedish prisoner, 1969

I was converted as an undergraduate at Cambridge ... when I was trying to think through what it *really* means to be a Christian, I found your book *Basic Christianity* absolutely invaluable.
From an Anglican minister

It was back in the fall of 1971 that I first heard of John Stott. Two years later, I had the privilege of meeting him as he spoke at an InterVarsity Christian Union meeting ... Truth is, from a human point of view, I owe my salvation to John Stott. It was reading his book *Basic Christianity*, in December of 1971 – the book had been given to me by a recently converted friend, my *best* friend. Reading it brought instant conviction of a gospel message I had until then (I was 18) felt unsophisticated and unnecessary ... the sense of peace was palpable. I never doubted I was saved, not then nor in the thirty-five years that have followed ...

From a professor of theology in the USA

I write today after finishing your book *Basic Christianity* and, in reference to that, I wish to thank you from the bottom of my heart.

Being twenty years old, I suppose that I am the product of a generation much filled with cynicism. Therefore, I looked entirely on the material and not on the moral to satisfy my needs and curiosities – of course, without fulfilment.

A young woman from Nottingham

NOTES

CHAPTER 1

1. Genesis 1:1; Hebrews 1:1–2; Luke 1:68.
2. Romans 1:1–4.
3. Psalm 19:1; Romans 1:19–20.
4. John 1:1, 14.
5. Matthew 1:21; 1 Timothy 1:15; Luke 19:10; Luke 15:3–7.
6. Psalm 14:2–3 (TNIV).
7. Hebrews 11:6.
8. Jeremiah 29:13.
9. P. Carnegie Simpson, *The Fact of Christ*, 1930; James Clarke edition, 1952, pp. 23, 24.

CHAPTER 2

1. For a discussion of the authenticity of the New Testament, see F. F. Bruce, *The New Testament Documents*, Inter-Varsity Press, 6th edition, 2000.
2. John 6:35 (TNIV); 8:12; 11:25–26 (TNIV); 14:6; Matthew 11:28–29.
3. Mark 8:29; John 8:56; 5:46; 5:39; Luke 24:27, 44.
4. Luke 4:18–19 (TNIV).
5. Matthew 11:28–30; John 6:35; 7:37.
6. John 6:29; 3:36; 8:24; 16:8–9.
7. Matthew 10:37; Luke 14:26 (TNIV).
8. John 15:26; 16:14 (TNIV).
9. Mark 1:15; 14:61–62; 8:27–29.
10. Luke 10:23–24; cf. Matthew 13:16–17.
11. John 5:17; 10:30; 14:11.
12. John 19:7.

13. John 8:19; 14:7; 12:45; 14:9; 12:44; 14:1; Mark 9:37; John 15:23; 5:23.
14. Mark 2:1–12; Luke 7:36–50.
15. John 6:35; 14:6; 11:25; 15:4–5; 4:10–15; Mark 10:17, 21; John 10:28; 17:2; 5:21.
16. Mark 6:2–3; John 7:15 (TNIV), 46; Luke 4:32 (TNIV); Matthew 7:28–29.
17. John 5:22, 28, 29; Matthew 25:31–46.
18. John 12:47–48; Matthew 10:32–33; 7:23.
19. John 6:35; 8:12; 11:25.
20. P. T. Forsyth, *This Life and the Next*, Independent Press, 1947.
21. C. S. Lewis, *Miracles*, HarperCollins, 2002.

CHAPTER 3

1. P. Carnegie Simpson, *The Fact of Christ*, 1930; James Clarke edition, 1952, pp. 19–22.
2. Tennyson, quoted by Carnegie Simpson, ibid., p. 62.
3. James Denney, *Studies in Theology*, Hodder and Stoughton, 9th edition, 1906, p. 41.
4. 1 Peter 1:19; 2:22; 1 John 1:8–10; 3:5.
5. 2 Corinthians 5:21; Hebrews 7:26; 4:15 (TNIV).
6. Matthew 27:24; Luke 23:13; Matthew 27:3–4; Luke 23:41, 47.

CHAPTER 4

1. We are not concerned here with the virgin birth of Jesus, for it is not used in the New Testament to demonstrate his Messiahship or deity, as is the resurrection. The case for the virgin birth is well argued in *The Virgin Birth* by John Gresham Machen, Lutterworth Press, 1958.
2. Following Henry Latham, *The Risen Master*, Leighton Bell, 1904.
3. This is clear from John's account of the burial clothes of Lazarus. For when Jesus resuscitated him, 'The dead man

came out, his hands and feet wrapped with strips of linen, and a cloth around his face' (11:44).
4. John 20:11–12; Matthew 28:6; Mark 16:6.

CHAPTER 5
1. Romans 3:22–23; 1 John 1:8, 10.
2. John 4:24 (TNIV).
3. Isaiah 29:13; Mark 7:6.
4. Mark 2:27.

CHAPTER 6
1. Isaiah 57:15 (TNIV); 1 Timothy 6:15–16; 1 John 1:5–6; Hebrews 12:29 (Deuteronomy 4:24); Isaiah 33:14; Habakkuk 1:13.
2. Exodus 3:1–6; Job 42:5–6; Isaiah 6:1–5; Ezekiel 1:26–28; Acts 9:1–9; 1 Corinthians 15:8; Revelation 1:9–17.
3. See, for instance, Matthew 25:30; Revelation 20:14–15; Luke 16:19–31.
4. Isaiah 59:1–2.
5. Mark 7:21–23 (TNIV).
6. Galatians 5:19–21.
7. Romans 6:17; Ephesians 2:3; Titus 3:3.
8. James 3:1–12 (TNIV).
9. Studdert Kennedy.
10. *Christianity and Social Order*, 1942; SCM Press edition, 1950, pp. 36–37.

CHAPTER 7
1. Matthew 1:21; Luke 19:10; 1 Timothy 1:15; 1 John 4:14.
2. John 3:16; Colossians 1:19–20.
3. Leviticus 17:11; Hebrews 9:22.
4. Zechariah 13:7; cf. Mark 14:27; Daniel 9:25–26; Isaiah 53; Luke 24:46.

5. Mark 8:31; Luke 12:50; John 17:1; 12:27–28; 18:11; Matthew 26:53–54.
6. Galatians 2:20; 6:14; 1 Corinthians 1:22–24; 2:2; 15:3.
7. Hebrews 9:26; Revelation 5:5, 6, 12.
8. 1 Peter 2:18–25.
9. Mark 10:45; Matthew 26:28.
10. 1 Corinthians 15:3; 1 Peter 3:18 (TNIV); 1 John 3:5.
11. Leviticus 5:17 (TNIV).
12. Leviticus 10:17; 16:22.
13. 1 Peter 1:2, 18, 19.
14. Galatians 2:21.

CHAPTER 8

1. See John 3:3–7 (TNIV).
2. 2 Corinthians 5:17, literally.
3. See John 16:7 (TNIV); 14:17.
4. See Acts 2:4; Ephesians 5:18; Romans 8:9 (TNIV).
5. Galatians 4:6; 1 Corinthians 6:19.
6. Matthew 28:19; 16:18.
7. Galatians 3:29.
8. Ephesians 4:3–4; Philippians 2:1; 2 Corinthians 13:14.

CHAPTER 9

1. Luke 14:28–30 (TNIV).
2. Mark 8:34–38 (TNIV).
3. Philippians 2:10–11.
4. Matthew 10:34, 37.
5. 2 Corinthians 6:14.
6. Mark 8:38; Matthew 10:32–33 (TNIV).
7. Mark 8:35–37.

CHAPTER 10

1. Revelation 3:20 (TNIV).
2. Proverbs 27:1; Hebrews 3:7–8.

CHAPTER 11

1. See, for example, Acts 17:28.
2. For our heavenly Father's care, see Matthew 6:7–13, 25–34 and 7:7–12, and for his discipline, Hebrews 12:3–11 (TNIV).
3. 1 John 5:10–12 (TNIV).
4. See also the systematic aids offered by the Navigators, Turner House, 54 The Avenue, Southampton SO17 1XQ, http://www.navigators.co.uk.
5. Romans 5:5; 8:15–16.
6. See Romans 8:9–17 (TNIV).
7. 1 John 1:9; 2:1–2 (TNIV).
8. 1 Peter 2:2.
9. Galatians 5:16, 22–23.
10. Organizations such as Scripture Union publish schemes and notes for various age groups and interests. Inter-Varsity Press publish for students and others *Search the Scriptures* (an advanced course lasting three years).
11. For instance, *The New Bible Commentary*, revised edition edited by D. A. Carson, R. T. France, J. A. Motyer and G. J. Wenham (Inter-Varsity Press, 1994), also available on CD as part of the IVP Bible Study Collection.
12. See, for instance, 2 Corinthians 6:14.
13. See, for example, 1 Peter 2:11; Philippians 3:20; 2 Corinthians 4:16–18.